Hawking God

HAWKING GOD

A Young Jewish Woman's Ordeal
in
Jews for Jesus

Ellen Kamentsky

Sapphire Press

Published by

Sapphire Press
P.O. Box 533
Medford, MA 02155

Cover art: William Grainge

Printed in the United States of America

ISBN 1-882459-00-8

Contents

Acknowledgements

My major debt is to my family whose love and support enabled me to leave Jews for Jesus and write this book. I am also grateful to David Clark, the staff at Unbound, the Cult Awareness Network, and all the people who supported my parents and me throughout my ordeal with Jews for Jesus. Special thanks also goes to my friend Deborah Carr and my professors at Boston University and Simmons College who helped me reclaim my life.

Many people were instrumental in making this book a reality. My friend Michael Prolman encouraged me to write the book and contributed numerous ideas on every level from technical to philosophical. Additional thanks to Rick Ross, Steven Hassan, Herb Rosedale, Hal Katzman, Rabbi Emily Lipof and professor Gerald Hickey. I also would like to thank Rabbi Moshe Halfon and Betty Silberman for their contributions to the "Glossary of Jewish Terms."

Preface

This book is about a woman who no longer exists. Six years ago I prayed to receive Jesus as my Lord and savior. Today I would not make that decision. As a Jew, I do not believe in Jesus and have no desire to be part of Jews for Jesus. This is the story of how despite these feelings I accepted Christ.

The good news is that today I am free from Jews for Jesus and have a satisfying life. The tragedy is that many talented, young people remain trapped in destructive religious organizations and cults. They have given their lives to an ideology that their precult identities would never have chosen. They are victims of mind control.

A few weeks ago, I was walking in Harvard Square--a place characterized by diversity and free thought--the perfect place for destructive cults to recruit members. I emerged from the subway, with a friend, anticipating Indian food. My appetite was spoiled by a Krishna selling cookbooks outside the subway entrance.

"Are you vegetarians?" he asked before introducing us to the real topic, Hare Krishna.

"No," I said, trying to remain calm and debating whether or not to debate him.

"Do you know about Hare Krishna?" he asked.

"I know the group is a cult," I replied.

"No," he said. "We are not a cult. We follow the *Bhagavad-Gita* like millions of people. Have you read it?"

"Believe me, I understand what you are and why you are doing this," I said. "I was a member of what I now regard as a destructive religious organization myself. I handed out tracts, across the street, over there," I said, pointing to a convenience store.

"You really should consider reading this yourself," he said, offering me a copy of the *Bhagavad-Gita.*

"No thank you. I'm not interested," I said, refusing to

touch his book. "Have you thought about what you are doing?"

"Yes," he said.

"Are you free to come and go as you please? Can you leave? Can you read anything you want?" I asked, hoping to get him to think about his situation for a moment.

"Yes," he said. "I am free, and I can read whatever I want."

"O.K.," I said. "Would you consider reading a copy of a book called *Combatting Cult Mind Control* by a man named Steve Hassan? Ask yourself if you could do that."

"We are not a cult," he said. "We are free to do what we want. I hope you will consider Hare Krishna."

I left him 99% sure that he would not read Hassan's book and 100% sure that I would not join Hare Krishna. Perhaps one day he will walk away from the Krishnas. Perhaps his family will hire an exit-counsellor. Hopefully one day he will be free.

My friend did not understand my concern.

"The guy's an idiot. He's stupid. Why do you care?" he said.

My friend's words upset me as much as the Krishna's had.

"Because, I was no different than he," I told my friend. "I thought I had the truth just like him and was determined to share it with people like you."

"No, not you--I can't believe it," he said.

Believe it. I too had stood on street corners. Hawking a different God, I handed out thousands of pamphlets and gathered hundreds of phone numbers praying that God would send open victims across my path. I was a religious fanatic. I believed all people who did not accept my truth were going to Hell. Mine was no nine to five calling. I was always on call, praying, preaching, looking for converts.

Jews for Jesus and groups like them exist and are a threat to Jewish identity. They are dying to drag Jews into their ranks. Jews for Jesus is a well-funded missionary machine actively recruiting Jewish people. They spend millions of dollars each year to win converts.

Christians, Jews, even people active in the anticult field don't know where to place Jews for Jesus. Members of the organization are masters of disguise. They hide their true nature (sometimes even from themselves) and present a carefully contrived image to the world. What do they believe? How do they operate? Are they Christians, Jews or both? What's wrong with what they are doing? I've written this book to help answer these questions and hopefully prevent people from going through what I did.

Groups like Jews for Jesus work by preying on our religious doubts and exploiting our insecurities. They seek simple answers to complex questions. They use dogmatism to produce certainty.

Today, I revere reasoning and celebrate my Jewishness. I hope this book encourages people to find and celebrate their own truth. I hope this story helps others uncover and fight destructive forces diverting that effort. Know yourself, discover your truth, so when someone approaches you hawking God, you can say, "Thank you very much, but I'm finding my own way."

Special Note To Reader

Many of the names in this book have been changed to protect individual identities.

1

Growing Up Learning to Bake Challah

On June 2, 1986, I recited a prayer that changed my life. My hair and eyes retained their same shade of brown, I held the same high-pressure job and occupied the same cramped apartment, but I believed everything was different. A transformation, encouraged and developed by members of an organization well-versed in the language of manipulation, had begun.

Today, six years later, I recall my years with Jews for Jesus. My mind is clear as I remember events that separated me from myself, my family and my world. Some memories are painful. Sometimes I want to forget and move on.

People question my involvement. "How could you?" they ask. Explaining is awkward, draining. Some individuals don't believe me; others don't understand. They see an articulate, happy woman, weeks away from a master's degree. Perhaps they feel invincible and cannot imagine my story happening to them.

Before I joined Jews for Jesus, my life was typical for a young, Jewish woman. I was born at the end of the baby boom. The first thirteen years of my life were spent in Ossining, New York, a medium-sized town about an hour from Manhattan. My parents, two brothers and I lived in a three-bedroom home complete with a playroom and spooky attic. In the evenings we'd play kick ball in the street or watch episodes of the Brady Bunch.

I was the first member of my family to be born in New York. The rest of the family was from Jersey. Both of my parents grew up in Newark within blocks of each other. My father lived behind a candy store where you could buy the latest issue of Superman and a chocolate malt for fifteen cents. My mother's family owned a small grocery store where they sold bottles of unhomogenized milk and soft, white bread.

My grandmothers were second generation Americans. My grandfathers left Russia in their teens to escape anti-Semitism. They brought Jewish identities with them and transferred religious traditions to their children. Unfortunately anti-Semitism followed them to America and afflicted my parents.

On Saturdays my father attended a Conservative shul where he learned to read Hebrew and studied for his Bar Mitzvah. Afternoons were spent shmoozing with aunts and uncles, cousins and grandparents. Although my mother's religious training was less rigorous, being Jewish was as much a part of her identity as being female.

Judaism was not just a religion. Judaism infused our lives like ivy wrapping its way about an ancient structure. I was weaned on chicken soup and named in synagogue. Today my political and ethical stances reflect my Jewish values.

Many of my fondest memories are of the Jewish holidays. Each Rosh Hashanah my mother would bake a large, raisin incrusted challah, and we would dip sliced apples in honey for a sweet new year. On Chanukah, we recalled the Maccabean miracle by eating latkes and lighting the menorah.

For my family, Judaism was rooted in the home. The mezuzah marked our house and reminded us of our faith. Whether we attended services, stayed home, or went to the movies, Friday night was Shabbes. We gathered as a family to bless candles, bread and wine, and enjoy a lovingly prepared meal.

Synagogue enlarged our faith and linked us to the Jewish community. I started Hebrew school in second grade. On the first day of class, the rabbi and cantor presented new pupils with a miniature Torah and a dab of honey to symbolize a sweet learning experience. I sang the Shema, baked challah and listened to Bible stories including Noah's Ark which left me wondering why the lions didn't eat all the other animals on the ship.

I never found out what happened to the animals. My questions were usually dismissed. "It's not important," my teachers replied. I forgot about the lions and learned to stop questioning. I could utter the words of the Hebrew Bible, but their meanings remained enigmatic.

My interest in Judaism blossomed as I studied for my Bat Mitzvah. The next year, I toured Israel with my parents. My Jewish roots emerged from the sand. Abraham, Isaac, Rebecca and Rachel had really existed. For the first time I was part of the majority. On Simchas Torah my parents and I danced in the streets of Tel Aviv with our fellow Jews hugging and passing Torahs between generations. Sukkahs, hung above our heads, reminded us of the Exodus. Vulnerable and threatened from the beginning, these Israelis celebrated their existence just miles away from neighbors wanting to annihilate them.

Although I never experienced the anti-Semitism faced by Israelis, Holocaust survivors and my parents, my ethnicity alienated me from Gentile peers. Usually there were only two or three other Jewish students in each of my classes. On Yom Kippur, the holiest day of the year, my parents kept me out of school, so I had to make up classes. During the winter I sang "Born in a Manger" and "Silent Night" although I was not a Christian and never celebrated Christmas.

At the University of Pennsylvania, where I went to college, many of my peers were Jewish, and I felt free to express my faith. Classes were canceled on the High Holidays and the dining hall served Kosher foods on Passover. Hillel held workshops, lectures, services and dances; off-beat, off-campus chavurahs welcomed visitors. Attending Sabbath services became a Friday night ritual for me, a time to relax and be with friends.

2

New York or Bust

The transition from college to career was difficult. I had always been in school. From age five to twenty-two my world consisted of books, studies, classmates and exams. Graduation emancipated me, but I wasn't ready for freedom. Teachers prepared me for employment, but no one warned me about life.

In the eighties, jobs were plentiful. I received several offers. When acceptance letters arrived from Bloomingdales and BATUS (British American Tobacco United States) Retail Group there was no doubt: I was going to New York.

After accepting BATUS's offer, I enjoyed the life of a second semester senior. Between parties and completing classes, I packed and prepared for New York. Memories of Broadway, the Metropolitan and Rockefeller Center stood out in my mind like birthday parties and trips to the zoo. New York was a wondrous place. New York was "The City."

I fantasized about living in Manhattan. After becoming an eminent force in the retail world, I would buy a posh apartment on Park Avenue West, eat in the trendiest restaurants and dance at the hottest clubs. Twice a year I would travel to Paris, London and Milan to discover the latest trend. On the weekends I would escape to the Hamptons or Martha's Vineyard.

My illusions were flattened by The City. Living in the Big Apple was everything I expected, but more blemished, lonely and stressful than I could handle. If I had known how difficult living in New York would be, I might have resided elsewhere.

Finding an apartment in The City was tough. There were no student dumps for $250 a month. "Cute" studios rented for

$750 and one bedrooms for $1,000. I ruled out living alone and joined a roommate service. Although the chances of finding decent housing improved, I now had to worry about getting along with a roommate.

The first potential roommate I met sold shoes for Bergdorf Goodman's. Her apartment, which was located in the Gramercy Park area, was beautiful--her personality was not. She made it clear that the space was her property.

"You have your own bedroom and bath. The rest of the rooms are off-limits, Ms. Kamentsky," she said.

Disappointing encounter followed disappointing encounter. Finding an apartment in a foreign country would have been easier. The experience depressed me.

I continued to call and hope. Two dozen conversations later, I found a promising lead. The apartment was in a nice neighborhood in a doorman building between 2nd and 3rd on 49th Street. My potential roommate sounded agreeable, so we arranged to meet.

I immediately liked Joni, although I had a few misgivings about her black nail polish. She was a part-time punk and full-time secretary, combing her ink-black mohawk down by day and lacquering it up with Aqua-net by night. We spent a few minutes discussing the apartment and living arrangements, and talked for hours about the fun we would have together. By the end of the conversation, I was sold on the idea of moving in with Joni and gladly ended my housing quest.

BATUS's executive training program started after the Fourth of July. On the first day of work, I joined a dozen nervous, Ivy-educated graduates for orientation. The distinguished looking CEO and director of personnel greeted us over muffins and coffee. A tour and training details followed.

Training was fun. I shopped the market, wrote reports on paisley and plaid and scrutinized copies of *Italian Vogue*. Trainees compared experiences, shared stories and soon became friends.

After three months, I was assigned to the home department. I was crushed. I wanted to work in ready-to-wear. My supervisor was as disappointed with me as I was with the position. I didn't care what breed of duck was used for down pillows, and I couldn't get excited about flannel sheets in August. My attitude showed in my work. Unable to satisfy my boss, I failed miserably.

I released my frustrations at night. With Joni as my companion, I was instantly hip. After performing lengthy beauty rituals and changing half a dozen times, we'd hail a cab and head to the Palladium. We never paid admission. Joni just smiled and we were in, while the B and C crowd waited in line delighted to pay the $20 cover.

Clubs quickly lost their appeal while work became frustrating and tedious. The men I met were shallow; the woman were vain, competitive and willing to slash stockings to win the boring men. The glamourous life I envisioned evaporated leaving only filthy New York pavement.

Change blasted through my life early in 1986. A small article in *Woman's Wear Daily* revealed that BATUS was disbanding. Anxiety buzzed through the office. No one knew what would follow. We soon learned that the changes would cost us our jobs.

The opportunity to exit gracefully was mine. I was elated. However delight was short lived. Uncertainty began to haunt me. In a few weeks I would be unemployed, and for the first time in my life I didn't know where I was going.

I vacillated and floundered. On Monday I wanted to move to Boston; on Tuesday I couldn't bear leaving New York; on Wednesday I contemplated becoming a stock broker; on Thursday I joked about driving a truck; on Friday I didn't know that to do. Want adds, resumes, cover letters and job agencies permeated my existence.

Saks Fifth Avenue, willing to absorb some of the BATUS trainees, interviewed me. I considered a position in men's accessories. Ties, suspenders and socks intrigued me, but not enough to work long hours on a retail floor.

After seven months in The City, I had a much clearer image of New York and retailing. Neither interested me. Three-quarters of each pay check went to sharing a one-bedroom apartment; a loaf of bread and bottle of milk cost $5.00; people were rude. Why was I living here?

I decided to end my affair with New York City and move back to Boston. I bought a copy of *What Color is Your Parachute* and began to read the classifieds section of the *Boston Globe*. Maybe I'd work for Greenpeace or raise funds for the Boston Ballet, I thought.

Joni wasn't happy about my decision. Sick of revolving roommates, she joined me in terminating the lease. We began to pack, not sure exactly where our bags would land.

3

New York Busts Me

When I was sixteen I pierced my ears, traded glasses for contacts and started wearing braces all in a week. Quick change is a personality trait. When I was twenty-three I stopped working for BATUS, jumped into a sales position and moved into a new apartment within twenty-four hours.

These decisions were made at the last minute in the name of love. It was a simple scenario: girl meets boy, girl falls for boy, girl finds job and stays in New York to be with boy.

His name was Paul. He put no pressure on me to stay in New York. But I was smitten and didn't want to stop seeing him.

Paul and I met in an after-hours club between Saturday night and Sunday morning in mid-February. I rarely stayed out so late, but with my life resembling a teeter totter, sleep seemed immaterial.

That night Joni and I left the Palladium at 2:00 a.m. The smell of oregano and burnt mozzarella caught us as we walked down 14th street.

"Let's stop for pizza," Joni said, escorting me into Ray's Pizzeria.

I treated, ordering two slices and a pair of diet cokes to cut the grease. Timmy, a displaced bartender from South Carolina, joined us just as we were about to burn the roof of our mouths.

The three of us complained about Manhattan and our love lives and tried to decide whether pizza was more a powerful aphrodisiac or anti-depressant. We each ordered another slice and discussed what to do next.

"Interested in going to Tories?" Timmy asked.

"Sure," Joni said, answering for both of us.

We left Ray's and walked east towards 3rd Avenue to hail a cab. A vacant vehicle stopped abruptly in front of us. I swallowed apprehensions about the club and slid in next to Joni. The door slammed sealing us in. Minutes later, jostled but unharmed, we arrived at Tories.

The club was filled with people and smoke. Upstairs, where we went for drinks and conversation, was quieter. Remaining virtually silent, I ordered water and tried to appear comfortable.

"Let's go downstairs, Joni," I said, moving towards the stairs.

Joni followed me as I headed towards a patch of empty space.

"Mind if we sit here?" I asked.

"No, not at all," the young man occupying part of the couch replied.

I took a seat and continued talking to the man.

"My name's Ellen," I said.

"I'm Paul," he replied.

Dressed in Levis and a flannel shirt, he looked normal, but aberrant against the hip crowd. The oppressive club dissolved as we talked. We could have been a couple of college coeds drinking beer from thin, plastic cups at a fraternity party instead of two urban professionals consumed by New York night life.

"Let's get out of here and get some breakfast," Paul suggested. "I can't leave my roommate," I replied, feeling cautious.

"She can take care of herself," he said, grabbing my hand and leading me into the sunshine.

In the light I felt exposed, disoriented, foreign. My outfit had lost its luster hours ago. I wanted to crawl into fleece-lined sweats and hide. I needed to walk, to breath, to take in the cool air.

The early Sunday morning street was quiet. The New York Times wasn't even for sale yet. Soon couples would be up making plans for brunch, a walk in Central Park or an impetuous trip to the beach.

"Where should we go?" Paul asked.

I suggested the Kiev. The restaurant, which served the best blintzes, peroges and French toast in town, came to mind immediately. I always felt comfortable there, and I knew the establishment would be open.

Paul and I walked down 2nd Avenue. We stopped briefly and kissed beneath some bare construction. Silence followed. I tried to piece together the events which were still unfolding.

The Kiev was empty. We sat down in front by a window. The waitress brought two coffees; I ordered a fruit salad. Brief conversation followed. I had trouble meeting Paul's gaze and focused on my coffee. The all-nighter had left me vulnerable, spent. I wanted to go home and rest.

Paul left money on the table, and we went outside to catch a cab. In a few minutes I was in front of my apartment. We exchanged numbers and parted.

"I'll give you a call," Paul promised.

Paul phoned the following Saturday and invited me out for dinner. I really wanted to see him and cancelled plans with Joni. She understood and probably had just as much fun without me.

Traveling to the restaurant, on the Upper West Side where we planned to meet, was a problem. There was no direct route. I either had to transfer trains twice or string together three bus routes. I opted for the subway and managed to get there in about an hour.

The trip across town became routine as I continued to see Paul several times a week. I was drawn to his intellect which awakened my own interests in philosophy and religion.

The romantic aspect of our relationship ended after several months, but we continued to spend time together. Paul became a mentor explaining concepts and helping me grasp new ideas. He never told me too much about his background or beliefs, but he was happy to answer my questions or point me towards self discovery.

Paul introduced me to two new topics: prayer and Christ. One afternoon I asked him if he had any suggestions. He thought for a moment and replied, "Yes, pray."

I found his response strange, but I took his advice. Apart from repeating words in synagogue, I had never prayed before. I wasn't quite sure how to start. I ignored prayer books and synagogue. My apartment became my sanctuary, my own words my prayers.

Paul suggested a few books including *The New Man* by Maurice Nicoll. The text had several chapters on prayer. The book, which discussed the New Testament, also introduced me to Jesus. As a Jew I had always felt uncomfortable thinking about Jesus, but Nicoll's New Age explanations of Christ's teachings intrigued me. The book, although far from Born Again theology, left me thinking about Christ. I bought a Christian Bible and continued to consider Jesus and experiment with prayer.

I renewed my library card and made frequent trips to a book store across the street from my apartment. Plato, Dante and Joseph Campbell caught my mind and became my new companions. I was motivated by the joy of discovery. There were no exams, no papers to write--only life to figure out. Most evenings, after work, I sat at my desk pouring over texts and trying to make sense of the world.

But knowledge gushed into my life like a monsoon and tore at my rickety belief structure. I couldn't handle the difficult questions raised by my studies. Why was I here? Was there more to life? What happens after death? Why do people suffer?

The sharpness of New York intensified my confusion. I stopped ignoring suffering and began to see pain. The amorphous lumps on the sidewalks took human form and haunted me. They were hungry and homeless; I felt insignificant and helpless. I wrote in my diary:

> Sometimes I think I'm losing my mind. What I'm thinking, feeling and experiencing makes no sense. And does it make any more sense to drop bombs, to watch children die in Ethiopia and to let human shells rot on the city pavements when across the street the Rockefellers build cement palaces?

I remember wandering in The Village shortly after Reagan bombed Grenada. That night, feeling confused and disoriented, I wrote another entry:

> It's 9:15 and the only thing that's real is the sound of my boots slapping against the pavement. I turn numb and cold, unable to comprehend reality juxtaposed to my world of buses, clubs and street lights. I force myself to eat just to make sure I am still alive. So tonight life goes on as usual. I'll sleep, wake, go to work and nothing will have changed.

I trudged home and climbed the five flights of stairs leading to my isolated apartment. I wanted help. I wanted to talk to a familiar voice. I wanted the anguish to disappear.

Desperate, I called my parents in Boston.

"I'm really upset," I cried. "I just can't handle life anymore; I don't know what to do."

My parents offered me an ear, but little comfort. Words alone were not going to help me. I prayed for the depression to end, put existential thoughts to bed, and escaped into sleep.

4

Revelation

The sound of a garbage truck compacting last night's trash indicated morning. I lay for a moment focusing on ceiling patterns painted by the sun. I stepped out of bed, gingerly touching a toe to the carpet as if to test water. My emotions were fine. I felt light. The depression was gone.

A single penetrating thought vaporized my blues: I was here because God created me. I didn't know where the idea came from. There was no burning bush, no angel of the Lord calling "Ellen, Ellen, take off your shoes."

I put on Nikes, a T-shirt and shorts and headed for the street. I didn't jog; I ran past buses and taxis, apartment buildings and banks. I felt like a paper kite floating miles above the cement. I drifted home, breathless.

The joy of that morning continued, and I began to explore my new faith. At first, I kept quiet about my belief for fear of being locked up. My father was one of the only people I shared my secret with. Several times a month he'd fly into New York for business. I'd meet him at his hotel, and we'd talk over plates of nori-maki and chirashi-zushi.

"Dad, God is real," I'd say, trying to verbalize my discovery. He'd listen without hearing me.

I continued to work and live in New York, adding prayer to my daily routine. I thanked God for everything: frozen yogurt, short subway waits, the rain. I asked Him to bless my business and began to read and memorize Psalms by carrying the words of David, Solomon and Moses with me to the office.

I worked for a leather sportswear manufacturer selling skirts and jackets to department stores like Bloomingdales and Neiman Marcus. Each day I dialed dozens of numbers hoping to talk buyers into the showroom. Faith and prayer increased confidence and clients. I attributed my success to God.

During this period coincidences appeared to inundate my life. Each episode strengthened my conviction that God was real. At work the telephone book would open to the exact page I needed. I found myself grabbing 50 envelops or 100 order forms--precisely the number I required.

One evening I was walking home from work thinking about Kay, my closest friend from high school, who was traveling around the world. Minutes later, I opened my mailbox and found a letter from her written weeks ago in Tahiti. The following day, I placed a cassette in my tape deck just as the song I was about to play came on the radio.

We all encounter coincidence. Why did I exalt it? Like an audience who chooses to view slight of hand as more than a trick, I chose to believe that my life was enchanted. Today I stop and consider coincidence. An obscure word comes over the radio just as I am reading the same word in a book. A friend calls as I think of her. The phenomenon is real, but it doesn't mean that God is trying to tell me something. My magical thinking laid the foundation for deception.

A few blissful weeks passed, and I felt the need to find people who shared my feelings about God. There was a small Reform synagogue on the West Side not far from my office; at the end of the week, I would attend services.

That Friday after work, I stopped at one of the ubiquitous Oriental markets, which dot the streets of New York like fire hydrants, to buy a salad. I found an empty bench in Union Square and dinned alfresco, sharing bits of pita bread with the pigeons.

The service started at 7:30. I slipped through the entrance and took an empty seat behind a row of elderly couples. The men wore white and blue kepot, the woman matched suits from B. Altmans. Organ music signaled silence and announced the entrance of the cantor and rabbi.

The service was as dead as the deceased congregants

whose names were etched on brass plaques nailed to the pews. I sunk into the deep, velvet covered seats and waited for the liturgy to end. I had felt closer to God among the trees and pigeons in the park. I left the sanctuary disappointed but not surprised by the lack of inspiration.

Passover was a few weeks later. I'd try services again. I made several inquiries about purchasing tickets for the holiday and decided to attend a seder at a Jewish community center.

The day before Passover the Garment District closed early. No one wanted to talk about shmattes while steaming pots of fragrant matzah ball soup were brewing at home. After work, I returned to my apartment to dispose of last-minute chometz. I scrubbed out my toaster oven, searched the cabinets for cookies and wiped up traces of flour. Closed boxes of pasta and crackers were bagged and shoved into a closet. I dusted myself off, dressed for services and tried not to think about how much I missed my family.

Alone, I took the Lexington Avenue subway to the seder. Alone, I picked up one ticket, entered the dining hall and sat down by myself. Each plate was set with a single piece of gefilte fish and a wine glass. A seder plate kept the flowers company. Several glass custard cups filled with salt water, and maror, parsley and horseradish were scattered around the table.

More guests arrived. Some sat at my table, and soon I didn't look so alone. I turned and tried to talk to the man to my left.

"Hi, my name's Ellen," I said, trying to appear confident and friendly.

"I'm Rick," he said.

Twenty questions followed. Our conversation was as dry as Vegas in July, but I was happy to have someone to talk to.

Just as Rick and I were running out of things to say to each other, an employee of the center came over to see if our table had any room. In keeping with a Jewish tradition, which advocates inviting hungry strangers to share the Passover meal, it was a custom of the center to ask people from low-income housing to join the seder. There was one empty seat.

"Do you mind if someone sits here?" the employee asked.

There appeared to be no problem until the guest arrived. He was black and lived in a residential hotel a few blocks from Herald Square. One woman at the table complained and refused to dine with our guest.

The display of hypocrisy disgusted me. I thought Judaism advocated compassion, but I saw racism and hatred. I felt ashamed and sad. Even four cups of Manischewitz failed to lift my mood.

Robot-like, I iterated the prayers, and with the ardor of someone eating sawdust, I swallowed the symbolic food. I refused to sing and couldn't wait to leave.

That evening the spirit of Elijah withdrew from the cold dining hall, and God remained a story book character in the pages of Exodus. I would look elsewhere for people to share my experience of God.

5

O Where, O Where is God?

New York felt like a Hell hole, but was it a Godless vacuum? Amidst the monarchs of Madison Avenue, the bums of the Bowery, and the wealth of Wall Street, there had to be people led by God. I would find them.

Suspending my apprehensions about Christianity, I visited a church. The congregation was close to my office and looked friendly and inviting. I often passed the building on my way home from work. Sometimes I stopped to admire the plants and byzantine architecture which stood out like an oasis, lush and serine, against the city.

Pushing my Jewish roots aside, I entered the garden. I walked past stone crucifixes and saints. The figures, familiar to me from art history, were foreign in Judaism.

Inside, the sanctuary was dark and cool. Tinted light, shining through the stained glass windows, shaded the mahogany pews. I took a seat and leafed through a Christian Bible.

"God, is this O.K.?" I asked. Silence pervaded.

I got up and walked past a confessional half expecting a white collared priest saying, "May the Lord be in your heart and on your mind," the way clergymen do in the movies. I rounded a corner and knocked on a closed door belonging to one of the ministers.

The man who greeted me didn't fit my stereotype. He was dressed in street clothes, and his office was lined with hundreds of books on subjects from religion to relationships.

"How can I help you?" he asked.

"I want to talk to someone," I said.

"What would you like to talk about?" he asked.

"Strange things have been happening to me," I said. "I

think it has something to do with God."

I continued to tell my story. I expected him to understand and end my confusion. Instead he listened attentively, sincerely appreciating what I had to say, but offered no resolution.

"Please feel free to stop by or join us for services," he said, and sent me away.

Back on the street again, I stayed out of synagogue and churches. If God created the universe, He certainly could direct me. But I wanted a quick fix and simple answers. I was a willing victim for anyone who could point me towards God and ease my loneliness. If another group had met my needs first, I would have placed my alliance with them instead of with Jews for Jesus.

My first encounter with someone who appeared to "know" God occurred while I was searching for plants, not spirituality. Spring had wet my appetite for African violets and daffodils, so I was easy prey for the hyacinths hanging out on 6th and 3rd, whose perfume lured me into the plant store.

I spent almost an hour among the flowers trying to figure out which plants would grow in my apartment. One of the men who worked in the store sensed my uncertainty and offered assistance. He steered me away from the miniature roses and suggested a day lily. Attracted by the graceful white flowers, I took his advice.

I paid for my plant and the man carefully wrapped it in plastic.

"God certainly creates beautiful things," I said.

"Yes, He does," the man replied. "I never run out of things to thank Him for while I'm working here."

Surprised to find someone talking about God in a personal way, I asked, "How long have you believed in God?"

"For almost twenty years," the man said.

I lost my interest in plants and became preoccupied with the man's faith. He told me how he had come to believe in Jesus and what God meant to him. I thanked him for talking with me and left the store confident that there were people in New York who believed in God.

My next meeting with a believer in Jesus was also unexpected. The encounter took place on a Greyhound bus pointed towards Cape Cod. The bus arrived; I took a seat and settled in with the latest issue of *Vogue*.

The bus was nearly full. I was not the only person anxious to escape the city.

"Is anyone sitting here?" a young woman asked me.

"No," I said, offering to hold the space while she secured her bags.

She sat down and sighed, "The Lord always provides."

There were those words again: "the Lord." The name the man in the plant store had used to refer to Jesus. I wondered if she shared his faith. I quickly found out. She reached into her bag and pulled out a Christian Bible, worn from prayer, inscribed with the gold letters "Maxine Parker."

I turned away from *Vogue* and glanced at her Christian Bible which was marked with yellow hi-lighter and black pen like a college text. She was reading First Corinthians, a chapter I hadn't dared to examine because it was in the New Testament.

"Where are you going?" I asked, wanting to talk about God, but too nervous to breach the subject.

"I'm visiting my sister in Providence. She's graduating this semester," she said.

"I'm going to Cape Cod," I said, realizing that we would be seat-mates for the next several hours.

"I missed the last bus," she said. "But I'm not worried about it. The Lord always has a reason for what He does."

Those words struck me again--"the Lord"--part of a secret code which I was not licensed to use. I envied Maxine's closeness to God. She dropped His name continually like a wife mentioning her husband. God kept her company at home and helped her at work and school. Apparently Maxine called on God for everything from faulty automobiles to renewed zeal.

"You ask God to help you on exams?" I asked, unable to believe that God cared whether she received an A or C in accounting.

"Sure," she said, turning to a passage in First Peter to support her claim. "Cast all your anxieties upon Him, because He cares for You," she read.

The bus arrived in Providence too quickly. I still had scores of questions. We exchanged numbers, she got off, and I continued my trip to Cape Cod.

That weekend, I didn't mention Maxine to my parents. I needed to relax. I wanted to swim in the ocean, not make waves. They wouldn't want to hear that I had been thinking about Jesus. The weather was glorious. I worshipped the sun and enjoyed the company of my parents. Why did I have to return to New York?

On Sunday I left the Cape. A few days later, Maxine called and left a message on my answering machine.

"Hi, Ellie," she said, unable to get my name right. "This is Maxine. I called to say hello and invite you to a Bible study at my house. I hope the Lord blesses your week."

I was happy and surprised to hear from her. New Yorkers rarely seemed to stay in touch, especially with strangers encountered on a bus. Maxine was abnormal--kind and friendly. That night I called her back. We exchanged stories about our trips, and I asked Maxine a few questions about prayer.

She answered joyfully (I could almost see her smiling over the phone) and sighted a few Christian Bible passages for me to read. Maxine told me about the study she was having and provided directions to her home in Brooklyn.

Saturday, before the Bible study, I visited a friend who lived on 161st Street. My friend, who was Jewish, was distressed by my sudden interest in Jesus.

"What are you doing studying the Bible on a Saturday night. Why don't you join me for dinner instead?" he asked.

"I'm not sure why I'm going," I said. "It's just something I feel I have to explore."

"This doesn't sound like such a great idea," he said.

Reluctantly he walked me to the subway station. A train approached, drowning our dialogue. I left him on the subway platform and never saw him again. He was the first of many people I alienated with my new beliefs.

I got on and attempted to read. The subway ride was long, leaving me time to get nervous. Forty-five minutes later, I arrived in Brooklyn. A train traveling back to Manhattan neared the platform. Did I really want to go through with this?

The exit sign beckoned. Two flights of stairs materialized. I found my way out of the station. The turn-style clicked behind me. I walked to Maxine's.

I was the first to arrive. Maxine took a few minutes to show me her basement-level apartment. It was filled with Christian paraphernalia: kitchen magnets which read, "I'm attracted to Jesus"; mugs with the words, "Jesus is my cup of tea"; and switches which read, "He's the light." She had hung a picture of Jesus over her bed like a teenage groupie paying homage to her favorite rock star.

"Ellie, did you forget your Bible?" Maxine asked.

"I guess, I did," I said, trying not to sound embarrassed.

"You should always carry it with you," she said. "I'll lend you one; what version do you use?"

"English," I said, not sure what she meant.

"Why don't you try the New American Standard. It's good for beginners," she said, handing me a Christian Bible marked with tabs so I could easily find the chapters.

Soon the other guests arrived, carrying Christian Bibles and wearing smiles. They did their best to make me feel welcome, but I found their over-friendliness disconcerting. A band of strangers were treating me as if we had been buddies for years.

The Bible study began with prayer. "Lord, we thank you for this evening of fellowship," Maxine began. "We ask that

Your presence would be with us here tonight. In Jesus name we pray."

A woman named Trish lead the study. She started by asking the group what God had done in their lives that week.

"The Lord finally got me a job," one man announced.

"I found a great apartment," said another.

"Isn't our Lord wonderful?" Trish asked, and began to tell us about how God was working in her life. She made a smooth transition from the stories to the study.

"This is a Scripture the Lord gave me the other day," she said. "Even so consider yourselves to be dead to sin, but alive to God in Jesus Christ," she read.

I tried to follow along, but couldn't find the passage. A ten minute explanation of the text followed. I didn't understand what she was talking about.

Trish finished preaching, and everyone joined hands. Maxine led us in another prayer, and people started crying, "Thank you Jesus," "Thank you Lord," "Help me Jesus." I kept quiet, unable to utter "Jesus" let alone pray to him. Everyone gathered around a young woman who had asked us to pray for her marriage. People touched her and uttered incomprehensible, garbled syllables without meaning.

I felt awkward and pretended to be part of the scene. The group was too engrossed to notice that I wasn't praying with them. I thanked God when the ordeal was over.

We adjourned to the kitchen for communion. Nonchalantly, I took a broken piece of matzah and a thimble-sized shot of grape juice. I followed the others, as they repeated "This is my body. This is my blood," trying not to choke.

The study finally ended. I had felt God's presence, but the talk about Jesus left me uncomfortable and confused. The meeting had lasted for several hours, it was dark, and I was scared to take the subway. I gratefully accepted a ride back to Manhattan.

After about ten minutes of kissing, hugging and promising

to pray for each other the crowd broke up. I walked to the car with the couple who was giving me a lift. They asked me what I had thought about the evening. I shared my apprehensions. The woman, who's name was Anne, was sympathetic, and she had a solution. Next Friday she promised to take me to a Jews for Jesus service. She assured me they would solve my problems.

6

I'm Born Again?

When Anne told me Jews for Jesus held their services four blocks from my apartment, I was amazed. Babe Ruth could have hit the office with a baseball, yet I couldn't recall passing the building. Three blocks up 3rd, hang a left on 31st Street and I was there five minutes quicker than you could order Chinese food.

The Friday night following Maxine's study, I walked to Jews for Jesus, determination overriding caution and the jitters. Like a detective researching a case, I would persevere until I had answers.

I had never met a Jew for Jesus and hadn't formed strong opinions about the group. My first encounter set me at ease. There were no crosses barring my path, no copies of the devotional magazine *Daily Bread* and no pictures of Jesus and the saints warning me, like a flashing red light, to proceed with caution. The scene was arranged to make me feel comfortable and welcome.

I arrived alone but was warmly greeted by a kipah-capped usher who handed me a Christian Bible and showed me a seat. The warmth, radiating about the room, was compelling and contagious. The woman seated next to me introduced herself and wished me a good Shabbes. Her distinct Brooklyn accent and Semitic features indicated that we were probably lantzmen.

Most of the congregation looked Jewish--even the non-Jews. Some of the Gentiles billed themselves as "spiritual Jews," linking their faith in Jesus with its Old Testament roots. In my travels with Jews for Jesus, I even met Gentiles who cloaked their true identities by wearing yarmulkes, speaking Hebrew, and developing a fondness for gefilte fish.

To the cognizant observer the hybrid of religions would have appeared as enigmatic as a sphinx. But I saw no paradox. My critical thinking was shrouded by vulnerabilities and a yearning for answers and friends.

The service started, and I found myself clapping, singing, and stomping to the music. The songs and prayers were familiar. Some were lifted straight from Judaism; the rest were infused with Yiddishkeit. Klezmer melodies and Hebrew words clung to the service like honey masking the Gospel and making it easier to swallow.

"Praised be Thou O Lord our God, Who has sanctified us by Thy commandments," became "Praised be Thou O Lord our God, Who has sanctified us in Jesus the Messiah." The change radically altered the original meaning.

The sermon and readings included passages from both the Torah and the New Testament, and the worship leaders called Jesus "Y'shua" (his Hebrew name meaning salvation). The Hebrew name slipped over the tongue like water, leaving no unpleasant aftertaste.

After the service everyone was invited to an Oneg Shabbat. There were no thimblefuls of grape juice or broken pieces of matzah. Instead one of the members of the congregation made a blessing over a challah, broke off a piece and passed the bread. A blessing over the wine followed and everyone broke up to shmooz and enjoy a host of snacks.

I grabbed a handful of grapes and approached the man who had lead the service.

"I was wondering if I could talk to you for a few minutes?" I asked.

"O.K.," he said, noticing that I was new. "Let's sit down over there," he said, pointing to several empty chairs.

He introduced himself as Yakov (not his birth name) and asked me how I had heard about the service. I told him about Anne and proceeded to reiterate my story. He listened intently. Like an expert jeweler evaluating a stone, he quickly appraised my situation and determined precisely where to set me.

"Do you have a minute?" he asked.

"Sure," I replied.

"I need to go downstairs," he explained.

We took the elevator to the first floor, and he opened a door leading to several offices. I watched him fumble through papers not sure what he was doing. He pulled out a date book and tried to schedule a visit with me.

"I don't know what nights I'm free," I said, seeing no reason to meet immediately. "I'd rather give you a call next week."

Like a salesman hungry for a commission, he insisted on scheduling a date, and we eventually agreed on a meeting time.

"I have to get back upstairs," he said. "I'm glad we had a chance to talk." He thanked me for coming to the service and walked me to the door.

I surprised Yakov by showing up the next day to help clean the office. Services were so enjoyable that I decided to join the cleaning party which had been mentioned during announcements. I spent my Saturday hunched over a soapy bucket of Ajax scrubbing floors, erasing fingerprints and whistling to gospel music.

I started working for the group even before I was enlisted. The draft was finalized during my next visit with Yakov. Before the visit, I joined his family and several members of Jews for Jesus for dinner. The warm meal and company surpassed my usual fare: canned tuna, lettuce and the newspaper.

Yakov introduced me to his wife, Mary. She was warm and friendly like Yakov. I decided to discuss some of my confusion with her.

"I understand that God is real and personal, but what's all this Jesus stuff?" I asked.

Yakov quickly ended my confusion. After dinner we went down to the office for a Bible study. Yakov recited a quick prayer before we started, asking God to open our hearts and minds. Prayer appeared to precede most activities.

He handed me a Christian Bible, and we turned to a verse in Isaiah. I read, and Yakov asked me who I thought the passage was referring to. I wasn't sure. Yakov showed me another verse, and he tried to build a case to show that Jesus was the Messiah. I wasn't convinced.

We turned to Isaiah 48, and I read, "And now the Lord God has sent Me and His Spirit."

"What do you think?" Yakov asked me.

"It looks like the Spirit of God, the Messiah and God are all one in this passage," I said. "This is pretty neat."

"Do you think that Jesus is God?" he asked.

"Maybe," I said. "The passage seems to show that God and the Messiah and the Spirit of God are all one, and the other passages we read looked like they were referring to Jesus."

Then he told me a prayer that people said when they believe in Jesus. I listened, not fully understanding the significance of what Yakov was telling me. But I wanted to be closer to God, and I wanted to be part of Jews for Jesus. I'd never really read the Bible before, and the prophecies appeared to show that Jesus was the Messiah. Praying to ask Jesus to be part of my life seemed the right thing to do.

The right thing to do? I made a commitment that took three years of my life, alienated me from the non-Christian world and devastated my family. I didn't even realize that I was converting. Like a teenager who starts smoking because gorgeous models advertising cigarettes look cool, I made an uneducated, uninformed decision. Smoking causes death! Conversion infected my soul, affected my future.

In a moment I prayed to receive Jesus. I became a Christian.

"God I know that I'm a sinner," I prayed out loud. "I believe that Jesus is the Messiah and that You sent him to die for me so I could be forgiven for my sins. Jesus please forgive me for my sins. Please come into my heart and be part of my life. God help me to live for you."

The prayer, according to the Gospel, made me a new creature in God's eyes, but I didn't feel any different. I could have been a murderer or a child molester; God had forgiven me. My place in Heaven was set.

Why did I sacrifice my intellect for this simplistic answer? Why did I let Jews for Jesus, an organization that I knew little about, determine the direction of my life?

Yakov, the triumphant midwife, immediately reached for the phone to broadcast my Born Again status. "There's someone I'd like you to talk to," he said, dialing San Francisco.

Why was he calling California? What was the big deal? Four rings reverberated over the conference phone. A man answered.

"Seth," Yakov said, "There's someone here I'd like you to speak with." Yakov nudged me towards the phone and encouraged me to tell the stranger about my prayer.

"Hello," I said.

"Tell him what you just did," Yakov repeated.

"I guess, I asked Jesus to be part of my life," I said, hoping that was what Yakov wanted me to say.

"Ellen, that's wonderful! Mazel tov," the stranger said, congratulating me as if I had discovered the cure for cancer.

Like a child taking her first steps, unaware of where walking will lead, I had no idea that I had begun a walk of faith which would change my life. The members of Jews for Jesus had clearer vision.

7

Learning to Walk, Where?

"Do you run?" Yakov asked me shortly after our first meeting.

"Yes. Why do you ask?" I said, surprised by his question.

"I've really wanted a running partner," he said. Perhaps I was an answer to his prayer.

We started covering the Christian Bible and the streets of New York. Several mornings a week Yakov would meet me at my apartment, and we would pursue "runner's high" and "higher truth."

Usually we jogged along the East River, observing gulls and shrunken Chinese gentleman practicing Ti Chi. Conversation was strained; exercise left us gasping for breath. Christian concepts left me distressed and confused. Accepting Jesus had been easy; embracing the dogma associated with following him was not.

"You mean everyone who doesn't believe in Jesus is going to Hell?" I asked Yakov one morning, unable to fathom that all the people I loved would spend eternity in Hades. "How could God do that?"

"What do you mean women are weaker vessels?" I protested, envisioning myself subordinated to a husband, condemned to a life of housework and children a la "Leave It To Beaver." I wanted a career. I was a feminist. I wanted no part of this.

"How can this be the only way to God? What about Buddhists? What about the Pygmies living in Africa who never heard the Gospel? Where do they go after death?"

My philosophical nature craved answers, but I made the mistake of seeking only one source for solutions--The

Christian Bible. "The Good Book" offered to settle all of my quandaries, if I accepted its explanations.

Using the Christian Bible, Yakov addressed each of my dilemmas. He pruned the doubts enabling Fundamentalist roots to take hold and strangle my former self. My old intellect and new faith fought; the two could not exist together. I trashed critical thinking and adopted Jews for Jesus' Born Again view.

I felt severed and began to cut myself off from the past. I stopped talking to old friends, took less interest in my job, and refused to listen to my family or speak with a rabbi. I started spending all my free time with Yakov and the other people at Jews for Jesus.

There was only one person in my life that I discussed my doubts with. His name was Greg, and he was also a new Jewish "believer" who shared my confusion.

We became close friends, visiting each other almost every day, spending hours talking about God and trying to decide if Jews for Jesus was legitimate. Greg had more misgivings than I. He felt that the group was demanding and was trying to gain control over our lives. He was uncomfortable with some of Jews for Jesus' aggressive tactics and preferred to quietly share the Gospel. Neither of us realized that in the future I would be executing those aggressive tactics.

Greg explored his faith, but he sought different avenues. He started attending church and stopped going to services every Friday night. He found other places to explore Christianity, and I no longer saw him at Jews for Jesus' Tuesday Bible study.

Yakov treated us differently. He spent less time with Greg and more time with me. Yakov asked me to work on window displays, accompany him on visits and distribute tracts. I spent most of my free time at the New York branch of Jews for Jesus; Greg joined a church.

Each morning after our run, Yakov and I would meet for bagels, banana and Christian Bible. We studied Christian scriptures, and I memorized Christian Bible verses.

Thoughts of prayer, fellowship and Christian Scripture seeped into my brain like chloroform. My view of reality was colored by Fundamentalist values. "It's as if you've pulled down a curtain," my mother, desperate to shake me out of my trance, remarked.

A few days into our studies Yakov taught me a new word, "Evangelism": the zealous preaching and dissemination of the Gospel. Yakov, a Vietnam vet who harbored a fondness for the military and Rambo, loved fighting for God. He relayed his enthusiasm by passing me a stack of gospel tracts and explaining how to win the race for souls. I took to the activity like a chocoholic takes to Godiva. I thought I was handing out tickets to Heaven.

My first sortie, a military term which Jews for Jesus adopted to refer to distributing gospel tracts, took place in upper Manhattan. Yakov assembled the troops at 0700 hours. Uniformed in T-shirts, imprinted with Jews for Jesus, and armed with pamphlets, we marched to the subway.

We disembarked near Museum Row at 79th and 5th a band of saints battling the "Evil One." Our defense was the armor of God; we covered ourselves in prayer and took up the shield of faith, the helmet of salvation and the sword of the spirit.

Yakov stationed some of his company on corners. The rest of us charged the streets. I hung with Yakov trying to imitate his maneuvers.

"Would you like one. Here you are. This is for you," I said, flashing a smile.

Battle was easy, exciting, fun. The only casualties were a few paper cuts and one lost warrior who took the wrong subway home. Victory, marked by the number of tracts handed out and phone numbers gathered, was assured. We were on God's side.

8

O Brother

On the home front a battle of faith was declared between my family and Jews for Jesus. The struggle was over my life, and for three years my parents and brothers never stopped loving me and hoping for my freedom.

Beholding my shell, inhabited by an alien who watched Jimmy Swaggert, must have been horrible. Drugs, prostitution, even a car accident would have been easier to handle. Terrible as these situations are, they have a course of action. There was no cure for Jews for Jesus, no detox clinic, no rehab center, no hospital to put me back together.

Like members of the Starship Enterprise, trying not to break the Prime Directive, my family couldn't decide whether to intervene. At twenty-three, I had a right to make my own decisions. But was I determining my destiny? The debate took them on a journey: to rabbis, experts on cults and destructive religious organizations, and to God.

My brother Howard was the first person to hear the "good news." Since childhood we had always confided in each other, sharing our adventures and misadventures. I thought he would be compassionate, but he did not receive the news with joy. Instead, even though he did not understand the implications of my decision, he became dismayed.

Howard came to town the week after I came to believe in Jesus. He was happy that I had stayed in New York because my residency gave him a reason to visit and a place to stay. Like a caged panther in the zoo, he had outgrown his home and was anxious to move. Manhattan was a refuge from the sameness of Buffalo where he lived.

He arrived Saturday morning needing a nap. I left him asleep on my futon and walked downtown to enjoy the Union

Square farmer's market. I wandered among the stalls and bought half a dozen banana walnut muffins.

When I came home Howard was up, impatient to explore the city.

"Where did you go?" he asked, annoyed by my disappearance.

"I got us some breakfast," I said, handing him a muffin, knowing food would assuage his temper and appetite.

We enjoyed a late breakfast and prepared to leave. I didn't care where we went. Shopping, museums, galleries, night life were losing their appeal. *Daily Bread* replaced *The New York Times* and church trips the Metropolitan Museum.

I let Howard pilot. Using a copy of *The Village Voice* to navigate, he steered us downtown. We wandered to Canal Street and poked through shops selling tinted plexiglass, copper coils, widgets and washers. Motorized by bins of gears, Howard's mind churned with ideas. Where I saw dusty junk, my brother, an artist, found treasures.

Trying to be patient, I watched him shop. Finally he was done, and I helped him carry the loot. It was early afternoon, and we headed over to Chinatown. We ducked into a noodle shop to enjoy plates of lo mein. Howard inspected his purchases over lunch, and we discussed how to spend the rest of the day.

We left Chinatown and the stench of fish, trying to avoid the discarded vegetables rotting under our feet. The streets took on another nationality as we passed Little Italy and moved on to The Village. Howard stopped at Unique Boutique to rummage through the racks with N.Y.U. students and high schoolers sporting the latest hair styles.

I watched, waited and worried. I had to tell Howard about my new beliefs but feared speaking to him. Informing him would be worse then having a safe sex talk with a new boyfriend. Yakov had offered to help me break the news, but I didn't feel comfortable introducing Yakov to my brother. To prepare myself, I reread the chapter in the *Growth Book*

Especially for New Jewish Believers entitled, "Relating to Unbelieving Family."

"Seek out the most sympathetic member of the family and explain that you've had a particular experience you'd like to tell him about," it said. "The decision to believe in Jesus as Messiah and Lord demands real commitment and a radical change on the part of the hearer. In fact, it can be threatening." At least I knew what to expect.

"Howard, I've been doing some reading," I started.

"What kind of reading?" he asked.

"It's a little like a synagogue group," I said. The people are really nice, and we get together and read."

"That's sounds interesting." he said, thinking that I meant a poetry group. "Did I tell you I might move to Boston?" he asked, changing the subject in time for me to change my mind about telling him that I believed in Jesus.

"No, Howard. When do you think you might leave Buffalo?"

"Sometime this summer," he said.

"That's great, Howard," I said, deciding this was not the time to share my news.

The moment of truth coincided with happy hour. We sat outside a cafe, enjoying the late afternoon. Our waiter brought chips and salsa; I ordered a Coke, and Howard had a Corona. Howard remarked at my choice of beverages.

"I don't drink much any more," I explained.

"Why not?" he asked.

"There are a lot of things that I don't do anymore," I said, preparing to unleash the Gospel.

"Like what?"

"I've stopped going to clubs," I said, as if to prove that my lifestyle had changed in a positive way.

"Did something happen between you and Joni?" he asked.

"No, it has nothing to do with Joni," I replied. "I started believing in Jesus."

"What do you mean, you started to believe in Jesus?" he

asked, visibly upset.

"I think he's the Messiah," I said, and then as I would do hundreds of times in the future, I attempted to illuminate another "unbeliever."

Howard wasn't interested in one iota of the salvation bit. As far as he was concerned Jesus was ruining his sister. He was already irritated because I didn't want to go to clubs and wondered how else my new craze would alter me and our relationship.

"Is this just another phase? Are you sure you know what you're getting into?" he asked so seriously that I almost laughed to dispel some of the tension between us.

"Yes," I said.

"Have you told mom and dad?"

"No," I said.

"You know they're going to be upset," he said.

I shrugged and stared into my soda.

"How are you going to tell them?" he asked.

"I didn't know."

Our conversation was interrupted by food. Howard ordered another beer; I studied my burrito and picked at the cheese. I felt empty yet had no appetite. Everything tasted bitter.

The food grew cold, and the meal was whisked away.

"How was your dinner?" the waiter asked, obviously not equating the uneaten food with displeasure.

"Fine," I mumbled.

"Can I get you some coffee or dessert?" he asked.

"No thanks," I replied. "Just the check, please."

Howard and I tried to put the meal behind us, but our relationship had been totaled. We headed East along 8th Avenue. The neighborhood grew hipper, and soon we were walking among a sea of people dressed in black.

Like a soldier on furlough, Howard was determined to enjoy himself despite my change in temperament.

"Do you want to go to a club?" he asked.

"Not really," I said. "I don't know if I can take it."

"Oh come on," he said. "Maybe you're making too big a deal out of this."

I finally conceded, and Howard began to scan the bars and his paper for bands. We passed the Pyramid Club and stopped to check out the Cat Club. Although it was only nine, the bar was filled with smoke and gyrating hips. Howard paid the cover charge. Immediately I wanted to leave. The music reminded me of a traffic jam and sounded like finger nails scraping along a blackboard. I imagined Satan in every corner laughing, manipulating dancers and driving people to drink. I had to leave. I pleaded with Howard over the noise, but he wouldn't listen to me. He had paid twenty dollars and wasn't about to miss the show.

Sick, scared and unsound I bolted through the door and ran uptown in my fancy, Italian flats. Half madwoman, half track star I arrived at my apartment breathless. Relieved, I bolted the door to keep out imaginary demons. Relief was short-lived. I felt guilty about leaving Howard. "What if he gets lost or runs into trouble?" I thought. I decided to wait up for him.

A few hours latter, the buzzer to my apartment alarmed me. I jumped from my chair. The buzzer rang again. Howard was impatient and waiting. Glad that he was home but scared of his temper, I hesitated and released the door. His steps grew louder with each flight until I heard him huffing at the door.

"What the Hell happened to you?" he demanded as I let him in. "Why did you run out of there? Do you know I wasn't even sure how to get back to your place? I don't know what's wrong with you."

Unable to defend myself, I remained silent.

"I'm still your brother," he said, as if to establish his place in my life. "Nothing can change that."

"I know," I said, feeling the pain of loss.

With nothing left to say, we hugged, but the physical gesture wasn't enough to bring us together.

9

Mother, I Can't Live Without Jesus

The photo album, in my parent's study, houses a picture of my mother taken two weeks after I entered Jews for Jesus. She's wearing a sharply tailored black and white suit and a smile. She almost looks happy. But her face is ashen and her eyes betray a lack of sleep. She has just found out that her only daughter is a Jew for Jesus.

I hadn't planned on telling her that weekend. Yakov advised me to wait. I would grow stronger in my faith, and Yakov would explain how to break the news. But my mother's intuition spoiled our strategy.

My parents travelled from Boston. I took a train from Grand Central, and we met in Dobbs Ferry, a small town outside of New York City. Our friend, Mike, picked me up at the station. My folks had already arrived at his house. They were waiting for me with Barbara, Mike's wife, looking as relaxed as the khaki pants they wore.

We enjoyed lunch on the patio followed by tall glasses of iced tea. I said little, focusing most of my attention on Porche, our host's cat. After lunch, I wandered about the yard praying and reading a carefully concealed Christian Bible.

My mother started looking for me.

"Ellen, Ellen," she called, waking me from my distanced state.

"Where did you go?" she asked, after finding me.

"I've just been relaxing," I said.

"We're going for a walk. Do you want to come?"

"I guess so."

Our friends lead us to a path along an aqueduct. I walked

ahead. My mother caught up with me, and we stopped to examine some grape vines. I offered her a tendril to taste. She declined, not confident with my knowledge of edible botany.

Barbara had more appetizing fare waiting at the house. After supper, we moved inside to escape the mosquitos and enjoy tea and talk. I said little, paid attention to the cat and excused myself shortly after the meal.

Upstairs a bedroom was waiting for me. I sat in a rocking chair reading my Christian Bible, the only book I had brought and felt I needed. Downstairs my father and Mike discussed business, while my mother and Barbara talked about me. My mother still remembers the conversation.

"Do you think Ellen's acting strangely?" my mother asked.

"I don't really know," Barbara replied.

"She seems depressed." my mother said.

"How have things been going for her in New York?"

"Truthfully, I don't think she's been having an easy time."

"Why don't you ask her if everything's all right?"

Taking Barbara's advise, my mother climbed the spiral staircase leading to my room and walked passed the watchful eye of the stuffed moose guarding the hallway. A moment later she knocked. Startled, I stuffed "The Good Book" under a pillow and opened the door.

"Hi, I just came up to visit," she said, sitting down next to me on the bed.

"Ellen, are you feeling all right? You seem a little depressed," she said.

I gazed away and focused on some book shelves across the room.

"Ellen, look at me," she said, grasping my shoulders.

I smiled nervously, just like I had with my brother when I told him about Jesus.

"Is something wrong?" she said.

"Mom you're not going to like what I'm going to tell you."

I was right. The words "I believe in Jesus" hit my mother like a rock shattering glass. Decades of anti-Semitic memories surfaced at the name Jesus.

"Think about what you're doing," she said, looking grim.

She didn't know what else to say and left me to deal with her sorrow. I felt cold, scared, hurt. I crawled under the quilt still crumpled from our conversation. Porche, the cat who had been waiting outside the door, jumped on the bed. I thought God had sent her as a sign to comfort me and fell asleep to the sound of purring.

Insomnia visited my mother that evening, and sleepless nights plagued her for months. The next morning her countenance was fit for a funeral, not the wedding she planned to attend. Not wanting to dampen anyone's spirit, she kept quiet. But watching her friend's daughter, a childhood playmate of mine also named Ellen, get married must have been agonizing. The ceremony underscored that my life was going in another direction.

Makeup and strong coffee helped disguise her mood. She even fooled my father and convinced him to let us walk alone.

"Ellen, I want to talk to you," she said, trying to exercise parental authority.

"Let's go for a walk."

"All right," I said.

We walked along the road unconcerned with our destination. My mother started the conversation where she had left it hanging the night before.

"Be yourself, think about what you are doing," she said. "I don't think you understand the extent of what you're getting involved with."

I replied with my nervous smile. I felt I was doing the right thing. I believed she didn't understand me because God chose to keep her unenlightened.

"Where have you been getting your information?" she asked.

"From the people at Jews for Jesus," I said.

"Don't you think you should question what they are telling you?" she asked.

"Mom, it's too late," I said. "I already made my decision. I can't live without Jesus."

10

Cape Bliss Crumbles

Ever since childhood I have seldom missed a summer on Cape Cod. Each year we would arrive at the shore eager to stretch our legs, examine the house, and dive into the sea. Apart from the car trip, which usually provoked nausea, the vacation was a delight. Until I joined Jews for Jesus, all disasters on the Cape were natural: beached whales, red tide, black flies and sun burn.

Cape bliss crumbled during the summer of 1986. The connection between my family and I disintegrated. I shattered my mother's heart, devastated my dad and depressed my brothers.

My mother summoned me to the Cape, shortly after my news about Jesus dropped, to discuss my decision. Her urgency eluded me. Jesus had solved all of my problems. Why would I want to examine my faith? My mother disagreed with me. Desperate, she resolved to rescue me.

Yakov advised me not to visit. I disregarded his advice. I wanted to shower my family with Christ's love. Stories of battles between parents and children filled my head, but I could not imagine my family pulling me away from Jesus.

I was wrong. While Jesus lulled me to sleep, my parents plotted and planned my exorcism. I lost my naivete. My parents grew smarter, sadder and more determined.

That summer our beautiful Cape house took on the atmosphere of a cancer ward. Everyone spoke in hushed voices and treated me as if I was dying.

"Ellen you seem so depressed. Do you want to talk?" my brother Lee asked, troubled by the changes he saw in me.

"Lee, I'm really fine," I said, wandering away to read the Christian Bible.

Later that weekend we went out to dinner together. The waiter brought us our menus. Lee sipped his water, ordered and continued to focus on the water. He wouldn't talk to me.

"What's wrong," I demanded. "Why won't you talk to me!"

"I can't help it," he said. "It's so sad. I can't believe what's happened to you."

He looked away and started to cry. The last time I had seen his tears, we were both children.

Like a terminally ill patient denying disease, I didn't understand why they were concerned. Obviously they didn't see God's joy, I thought. Truthfully, they were the enlightened ones. I was behaving strangely. The Ellen they knew and loved had left.

My family tried to contact me from beyond the grave where I had buried my personality. But like a drug addict on heroin, I refused to acknowledge that I had problems and needed help. I wouldn't consider other views or listen to anyone not associated with Jews for Jesus. I wanted to stay high on Jesus.

The phone awakened me from oblivion. Greg, my friend from New York, needed to talk with me. He sensed that my parents were going to attack my faith and called to warn me. I reassured him that I was all right, but the conversation spooked me.

While my mother was busy in the garden planting lettuce and tending tomatoes, I searched the house. In a few minutes I found evidence to validate Greg's hunch. Hidden in my mother's dresser drawer was a list of rabbis, therapists and groups such as the American Family Foundation and the Cult Awareness Network. On another piece of paper my mother had written my thoughts, feelings, behavior and actions.

I felt scared, betrayed, ambushed. I panicked and called Yakov. The secretary put me on hold. I waited on the line and watched my mother turn over the soil.

"I should have listened to Yakov. Why had I left New

York? How was God going to help me?" I asked myself.

Finally Yakov answered. I told my story; he quieted me; we devised a plan. I consulted a bus schedule. The next bus arrived in two hours, but the stop was at least a mile away. I felt trapped like a victim in a B-horror movie; any minute, I expected my mother to come bursting through the door. Yakov urged me to remain calm and get out of the house. He prayed for me and hung up.

Still shaking, I grabbed a duffel bag and started stuffing it with belongings. Upstairs I heard a door slam indicating that my mother was in the house. Trying to hide my fear, I asked her if she was going to town.

"Well I wasn't really planning on going," she said.

"Don't you need to go to the dump?" I asked.

"The garbage is getting full," she said. "I suppose I could go."

"I'd be happy to help you dump the trash," I said, trying not to sound too enthusiastic.

"All right, maybe we can go before dinner," she replied.

"Let's go now and get it over with."

"I was planning on going for a swim," my mother said.

"Why don't we get rid of the trash and go to the ocean afterwards?"

"I suppose that would be O.K."

"Great, I'll put on my bathing suit."

I ran downstairs, grabbed my bag and stole out to the car. The trunk was unlocked, and I stashed my stuff with the poise of a thief. I retraced my steps and joined my mother in the kitchen.

I watched my mother wash her tomatoes, praying that she wouldn't notice that my heart was about to break through my chest. I had less than an hour to get to town. Finally the vegetables were deposited in the refrigerator. We could go.

I followed her to the car, praying that she wouldn't notice my bag. She went right for the door; I breathed a sigh of relief and sat down next to her. I prayed silently. She drove.

At the dump, we each grabbed a handle of the trash barrel. Refuse cascaded down the rubbish pile; the garbage can followed. The lost trash can upset my mother. The lost time upset me. She tried to fish it out. I started to yell.

"Just leave it."

"What do you mean? It's a brand new trash can."

"We'll come back for it latter," I said.

Surprisingly, she listened to me and got in the car. In a few minutes we were in town by the bank. I waited with her in line as she withdrew the hundred dollars that she had promised me to cover travel expenses. I thanked her for the money and walked to the car. In one movement I opened the trunk, seized my bag, and made for the bus stop minutes before my get-away bus arrived.

My mother froze.

"What are you doing?" she demanded, almost too shocked to speak. I explained that I couldn't explain and had to leave. Desperate and unconcerned with her surroundings she started to yell at me in the middle of the quaint New England town.

"I'd throw myself in front of that car for you," she cried. "Don't do this!"

Her tears sloshed me in the face. I retreated and let the bus pass. The bag went back in the car. We drove without a word.

At home my mother ordered me to sit down.

"What are you doing? This isn't like you. Do you see what you are doing to us. I've never seen anything like this," she yelled, despite an effort to remain calm.

My mother tried to communicate, but I had become an irrational, frightened creature. There could be no peace, no understanding, only love. My family had failed to free me. I returned to New York and turned to Jesus.

11

Zombie for Jesus

Life in New York was becoming more difficult. I disliked my job and no longer wanted to sacrifice my life to the gods of glamour, culture and style.

Each morning I asked God to help me through the day. My new Born Again Christian sensibilities made it even harder to cope with a boss who abused his wife and swore like a teenage gang member. I found company business practices incorrigible. I decided to quit.

For the second time that year I was unemployed and confused. This time I was on my own. Jews for Jesus used the cross to slash the parental safety net. My parents were not funding Fundamentalism. They tried to persuade me to leave New York and renounce Jesus. I would vacate New York, but I would not forsake Jesus.

Support came in the form of advice and prayer. This didn't help pay the rent. Yakov, worried that moving closer to my parents would endanger my faith, urged me to stay in New York. My parents, worried that Jews for Jesus was endangering my life, encouraged a move to Boston. I asked God for help and had other's pray for me, but the Lord didn't answer. Either I wasn't praying properly or God was leaving me to my own devises.

Yakov explained that "walking" with God was like driving a car. "You step on the gas and let Him steer." Fueled by worries, I floored the pedal and pounded the pavement. I filled out applications, talked to mangers, and auditioned for positions at the hottest new cafes. Since I was either inexperienced or overqualified, responses were a mixture of, "Why would you want to work here?" and "We can't use you."

July 1st came. I paid the rent, continued to search for jobs, and considered getting a roommate. The idea of sharing two tiny rooms in an overcrowded city was distasteful. Instead of advertising for a roommate, I advertised to sublet. A few apartment hunters spotted my ad, tracked me down, and considered bagging the place. The prize went to an Englishman who offered his passport and $2,000 for security. I accepted his offer and arranged for him to take over the lease.

Bags were packed, furniture was sold, plans to settle in Boston were made. Between foraging for boxes and arranging to ship belongings, I visited Jews for Jesus. The scene was set for deeper indoctrination.

Two weeks notice at my sales position elapsed; Jews for Jesus prepared for Summer Campaign. I had time. Summer Campaign had room for a volunteer.

Summer campaign is a radical effort to tell Jewish people about Jesus. Each Summer twenty or thirty energetic "Jewish people," hungry to preach the Gospel, descend on New York. Dressed in blue and white T-shirts they explode on the streets in a flurry of gospel tracts. Quicker than you can say "Good morning, would you like one," they hand out their literature.

The average day begins at dawn. Commuters receive a plastic grin and a paper brochure from campaigners. After two hours of distributing tracts, often in dank subway holes, campaigners return to the Jews for Jesus office for breakfast and spiritual refreshment. Then it's out to the streets for another two hours of pushing paper. Lunch, a nap, and more tract distribution follow. If you've made it this far you get dinner and the privilege of going on another sortie. After two to three thousand tracts for the day, you collapse.

Why was I attracted to such nonsense? The campaigners enthusiasm, zeal, and friendliness roped me in. I wanted to join their party and they were glad to have me as a member. Initially I wanted to help as a steward by cleaning rooms or cooking meals. But when I approached Yakov to volunteer he handed me a tract bag and sent me out on the street with the rest of the campaigners.

My new friends tied up my time and dissolved my doubts. They encouraged my faith and left me little space to reflect.

"I had questions too when I was a new believer," my friend Lisa said. "But I kept believing and telling people about Jesus and my doubts went away."

Lisa was right. Persuading others reinforced my faith. I was committed to my decision, but I had doubts. Instead of exploring the doubts, I overcame them and strengthened my faith by selling Jesus to others. Why would I stand on a street corner telling people about Jesus if I didn't believe the Gospel? Why would I share a lie?

Distributing tracts was physically draining, but required minimal mental effort. As the campaign progressed, I grew tired and less able to think clearly. I switched to automatic and learned to recapitulate the Gospel in 25 words or less. I became a zombie for Jesus.

One sortie led to another. Soon I was distributing tracts three or four times a day five or six days a week. I met a Born Again punk rocker, a member of Models for Christ and a Yeshiva student who threatened me with his Talmud. Beneath the blaring lights and horns of Time Square, I gave tracts to pimps and pushers and prayed with an alcoholic to receive Jesus.

On a Friday, near the end of the campaign, I was broadsiding (a Jews for Jesus term for handing out tracts) on the corner of 5th and 42nd Street. An older man approached me. Like a porcupine, I bristled and prepared to defend myself. He smiled, and my adrenaline rush evaporated. I recognized him from Jews for Jesus and said hello. He offered a word of encouragement and asked if I was going to the baptism that night.

Baptism? No one had mentioned the subject. Did I need to get baptized? After my sortie, I found Yakov and told him about my conversation on the street. He apologized for his oversight and recommended that I get baptized myself.

I traded my T-shirt for a dress and prepared for services. The sanctuary was packed with people eager to support the campaigners and catch their enthusiasm. Some campaigners went out for the Friday night sortie, others shared victory stories, asked for prayer and enjoyed a night away from the battle.

Following services loads of people drove out to Brighton Beach for the baptism. I was to be immersed in the Atlantic on the shores where my ancestors had vacationed after fleeing Russia. I stood, preparing to proclaim my faith in Jesus, where they had celebrated their lives as American Jews.

Tom, a senior staff member of Jews for Jesus, explained the significance of Baptism. Baptism, he said, was an outward way to affirm and proclaim the inward commitment to Jesus that we had already made. Tom read a few passages from the Christian Bible and lead us in prayer and into the water. I watched as several other new believers were dunked including my friend Greg.

Finally it was my turn. I waded in up to my thighs and prepared to be immersed. Tom told me to hold my breath. "One, two, three," he counted and pushed me into the sea. Seconds later I rose, now an official member of the club.

I received an 8x11 certificate, suitable for framing, joyfully proclaiming:

> Ellen Kamentsky has joined the community of believers in confessing faith in the redemption of the God of Abraham, Isaac and Jacob. Ellen has demonstrated obedience to the lordship of Y'shua Hamashiach by the public act of receiving immersion in His name. His death, burial and resurrection is thus symbolized on this date. July 25, 1986

How easily I gave away the freedom and heritage that my ancestors had risked everything for.

12

Few Are Chosen

The campaigners handed out their last tracts, and I walked down my apartment steps one final time. Family and finances swayed me; I was leaving New York. There would be no more runs along the East River, no more sorties in Central Park, no more Yakov. Only Boston.

I made friends quickly. Two of the campaigners that I had met in New York lived in Boston. There was Neal, an aspiring young star eager to marry and rise in the ranks of Jews for Jesus. His odd couple roommate, Bob, was on a different path. Through sleet and rain and hail and snow he passed out tracts like a postman delivering letters from God.

My roommate, Susan, was the Boston branch office manager of Jews for Jesus. A math major from Tufts, she became a believer about a year before me. At times I felt she regretted her decision. She was too bright to be filing, taking dictation and answering phones. She missed her college friends; the days of partying were over for both of us.

Susan, Neal, Bob and I joked about being Messianic yuppies. We went on dinner dates sans wine and romance and spent hours complaining, criticizing sexy films (and seeing them anyway), playing Trivial Pursuit, and dissolving our frustrations in bowls of ice cream.

College students often gain ten pounds during their Freshman year; members of destructive religious organizations often put on twenty. I was no exception. Food was one of the few sensual pleasures allowed. I became heavier. The excess weight obscured my body and deflected suitors. As a Born Again Christian, I didn't want men looking at my body. As a hopeful missionary, I wasn't interested in finding a mate because a husband could end my calling.

Susan and I moved in together in the Fall. I had planned to live with my brother Howard, who had just relocated to Boston, but decided against it. Although our living situation would have provided great material for a sitcom, I knew we were not compatible.

Compatibility was not a problem with Susan. We got along fine, but we had trouble finding a stable third roommate. Nice Christian girls did not want to live in our cold, ugly, roach infested apartment. We went through three roommates in seven months.

The neighbors presented another problem. They were members of a cult called "The Boston Church of Christ." While I induced Jews to believe in Jesus, they held their own crusades. Like politicians trying to win votes, they were persistent in their search for converts. They disguised themselves as fellow believers, and seduced us with pancake breakfasts, spaghetti dinners, Bible studies and games of scrabble. They spoke Christianese, carried Christian Bibles, attended church--I thought they were Christians.

They were soooo friendly and tooo nice. "Hi, how are you, good to see you," they'd gush. One member kept visiting me at work. Next she invited me to lunch. I accepted. I was interested in developing a friendship; she had other plans.

We met at "the Garage" in Harvard Square.

"Ellen, I'm so glad that we could get together," she said.

"Yeh, it's great to have some fellowship in the middle of the day," I said.

"Don't you think it's interesting that God made us neighbors?"

"Yes. It's really nice having believers next door."

"Ellen, there's something I've been wanting to talk to you about."

"What's that?"

"Well, I wanted to know, have you been baptized?"

"Of course. I was baptized in the Atlantic Ocean. It was a

really wonderful experience."

"You really need to be baptized in our church."

"I don't understand what you mean. Baptism is symbolic. What differences does it make where you are baptized?"

"Ellen, unless you're baptized in our church, you're not saved."

I nearly choked on my turkey sandwich. I could recite the sinner's prayer backwards, forwards and sideways, had prayed with people to receive Jesus, and could provide an exact date for my own conversion; and she was telling me I wasn't "saved."

Her blind faith and need to convert me were very close to my own misguided beliefs and need to proselytize. I thanked her for her concern, assured both of us that I was "saved," finished my sandwich, and continued my own brand of evangelism.

I handed out tracts frequently and dreamed of devoting my life to evangelism. To pay the bills I worked as a salesperson for Crate & Barrel. Between dusting fixtures, folding fabric and ordering place mats I witnessed to other employees. I was careful; I was being paid to sell products not proselytize.

Days off were filled with evangelism. Neal, Bob and Chaim, the Boston branch leader of Jews for Jesus, were happy to take me broadsiding. Chaim did not treat me like Yakov had. Yakov was permissive and playful; Chaim was strict and serious. He ran a tight branch and expected me to march to his beat. This was the price of being accepted and considered for a staff position.

Members of Jews for Jesus discipled me: we studied the books of the Christian Bible; discussed Christian concepts of prayer, fellowship and salvation; memorized Christian Bible verses. Members of the ministry developed my witnessing skills, followed my progress and discussed where to place me. I wanted to be a missionary, but I was too young a believer for the job. Maybe I could sing with the "Liberated Wailing Wall," Jews for Jesus' Messianic gospel group, or work as an office manager.

My voice wasn't sweet enough for the "Liberated Wailing Wall," so I was tested to see if I was suitable for secretarial work. I buried my ivy league B.A., ignored my spelling ineptitude and agreed to the trial. I practiced typing and bought a spelling book, but only divine intervention would enable me to pass the examination.

I was tested. The results went to Jews for Jesus headquarters in San Francisco. They made an exception in my case. It was not God's will for me to be a secretary. Jews for Jesus wanted me to interview for a position as a missionary.

Chaim told me the news. I was delighted. I was willing to do anything for the ministry, but I didn't want to be a secretary.

I flew out to California with Chaim for the next council meeting. Beth, a friend from campaign, housed me. She was the ministry's art director but wanted to be a missionary. I understood her yearnings. Missionary life was exciting and promised heavenly rewards. Who wouldn't want to be a missionary?

Thoughts of declaring God's glory and confronting Satan danced in my head as I prepared for the council. I would tell them I loved God and felt called to do His work. Surely they would see I was missionary material.

Senior missionaries and missionary candidates arrived the night before the council meeting. The scene resembled a family reunion. The brothers (only one woman served as a senior missionary) hugged and hung-out, happy to be together.

The meeting began the following morning after breakfast, prayer and worship. The council discussed where to send workers and whether to open new branches.

They kept candidates nervous by not revealing when we were to be interviewed.

Finally the moment arrived. I said a final prayer and entered the meeting. Many of the faces surrounding me were friendly, but the atmosphere was not. Like a pledge at a fraternity hazing I was asked intimidating questions. Tom grilled me on the America's Cup Race because I had mentioned in my application that I sailed. Moishe Rosen, the director of Jews for Jesus, asked why I was always late and why I couldn't spell. They weren't interested in my faith. They wanted to divine vulnerability and define malleability.

I caved in, acknowledged my shortcomings, and promised to work on my weaknesses. Seth, who headed recruiting, asked me where I wanted to serve. Like a contestant on "Jeopardy" I fired back, "Wherever God wants me to be."

The council decided my fate. I waited. The other candidate hadn't made it. He wasn't missionary material. He was going home. "What would I do if they didn't want me?" I thought. I was too nervous to pray.

Yakov entered my waiting room. His smile dissolved my doubts. I was in. I was going to be a missionary with Jews for Jesus. I rejoiced.

I rejoined the council. They relayed their unanimous decision and welcomed me on staff. I was to settle my accounts in Boston and prepare to leave for L.A.

13

California Here I Come

I was on staff! I felt like I had just won the lottery. I couldn't wait to share the good news. I would tell mom and dad, Lee and Howard, Neal and Bob and ...

Chaim stopped me mid-sentence, before we landed in Boston. He warned me not to share the information with the world. I should tell people about Jesus and keep the council's decision to myself.

Your parents may make a scene and try to stop you, he explained. (I imagined my mother throwing herself in front of the plane to keep me from going to California.) The pain you will cause each other from a confrontation may scar your relationship forever, he told me. He may have been right, but sneaking away was wrong.

For weeks I kept the information from my family. I wanted to tell them about my position with Jews for Jesus. I wanted them to know I was moving to L.A. I wanted their approval. I wanted to say good-bye.

In my dreams my entire family was "saved." "Ellen, we are so proud of you. We always hoped one of our children would grow up and become a missionary," my mother would say.

Harvard Square was the last place I saw my mother before I was shipped away. That day grassy spaces were filled with truants playing frisbee and sunbathing. The weather was charged with promise; my mother was filled with hope. Maybe today she would penetrate my fog.

She entered Crate & Barrel as I dusted a row of stemware. "Hey, perfect timing," I said, when she appeared. "I was just finishing up. I'll be right back," I said, leaving her to admire dinner plates and flatware.

I grabbed my purse and followed my mother to the door. Out on the street I tasted a rush of Spring. In L.A., beautiful days would be as common as blonds.

We passed Ann Taylor and stopped to admire a pair of pumps.

"Let's go in," my mother suggested. I followed her, relishing the fresh, pastel suits and a moment of closeness. We were actually enjoying each other's company.

The warmth suggested an outdoor cafe, but we ditched the sun and entered a basement coffee house. The interior was dark and cool. We sat at an embossed copper table and studied the menu to the sound of Arabic music. Our waiter brought water; we ordered hummus. I'd miss meals with my mother, I thought.

Five minutes passed and then ten. How long could it take to fix hummus? My lunch break was almost over. To add to my anxiety, my mother decided to bring up Jews for Jesus.

"Ellen, I'm concerned that you've been spending too much time with Jews for Jesus. Maybe you should take a break from this," she said.

Annoyed at her for spoiling our last moments together I lashed out, "I'm going to be more deeply involved."

I left her with the check and uneaten food not sure when I would see her again. She left upset, but unaware of my plans. I had taken Chaim's advice. Soon I would be safe.

The game of tug of war was on. Both contenders were determined to win. There was no rest or neutral territory. Jews for Jesus couldn't cut the umbilical cord, so they lengthened the rope and planted mines to sabotage my family's love.

The idea of moving three thousand miles across the country without saying good-bye ripped me apart. "What kind of God would want me to do this?" I thought, preparing to break the fifth commandment: "Honor thy father and mother." Jesus restated the commandment in the New Testament. But Jesus also said, "He who loves father or mother more than

Me is not worthy of Me." I was confused.

My friends at Jews for Jesus explained everything. Their will supplanted and became God's will for my life. I was too young in "the faith" to know "the ways of the Lord." My superiors had "walked" with God for years. I trusted them, although their advice violated my gut, my family and one of the Ten Commandments.

The group provided help and direction as long as I followed orders. Assistance appeared, from L.A., in the form of a woman named Heidi. She phoned practically every day and invited me to call her whenever I needed to. She alleviated anxiety, addressed problems, answered questions and assured me that everyone in L.A. was looking forward to my arrival. She reminded me that I already knew Lisa and Jeff and told me Lisa would house me.

I trusted and confided in Heidi. She cautioned me not to seek help from anyone else. She would take care of everything.

Like an actress eyeing Hollywood, I started looking forward to my trip. Neal and Bob, both former L.A. missionaries, pumped up my expectations. I would broadside the beach, eat oranges from the trees and sun-bathe year round. I couldn't wait to leave Boston.

Instead of saying good-bye to my family, I would leave loving memories. I wove my feelings into a quilt. For weeks I gathered scraps of fabric and pieced together my feelings. When I had enough cloth, I cut up the remnants, laid out the squares, and sewed them together. The creation was one of the most beautiful things I have ever made. I hoped the patch work would bring peace.

I gave the quilt to my mother for her birthday. She was excited because the work showed that the old Ellen, who loved art and dance and knowledge and literature, was alive. Perhaps the most coveted gift, my freedom from Jews for Jesus, was possible. But after I left Boston, the quilt and my identity were enshrined.

One member of the family needed to know my plans. I decided to tell Howard.

We met, the day before my departure, at a sub shop near Howard's studio. That day nothing appealed to me. The olives, feta cheese and iceberg lettuce on my plate attracted only flies.

I swallowed air and prepared to tell him. Revealing my plans was worse than disclosing my faith. The information oppressed him. My crush on Jesus, which Howard saw as a phase, had become a love affair. Howard had enough troubles. My news exacerbated his pain. Howard's response resembled his initial reaction to my faith.

"You know what this will do to mom and dad," he said. Yes, we both knew what my decision for Jesus would do to them.

I turned my back on Howard and the chance at a normal life. Boston held nothing for me. Greyhound had picked up my bags to ship to L.A., and my old relationships were smashed.

I don't remember who drove me to the airport. A member of the Boston branch probably took me to the terminal. I just wanted to get on my plane and fly away.

Howard kept my secret, and my flight took off without a spectacle. In a few hours I arrived in L.A., my missionary field, and one of the largest Jewish populations in the world. Hundreds of people waited to be "saved."

Heidi met me at the airport, slinging a tract bag, fresh from a sortie herself. She was smaller then I expected, but her height had no bearing on her stature. Heidi was tough.

We waited for my bags and my bicycle. Heidi saw the bike and blew up. I had neglected to tell her about the additional item. I did not see any reason to. What was the point?

Obviously I had been wrong. She treated my small oversight like a major crisis. I half expected her to say, "Just wait until I get you home, young lady." Five minutes in L.A.

and I was already in trouble.

I was upset about leaving Boston and didn't need this. I felt like a shoplifter who has been condemned to life imprisonment for stealing a bag of gum drops. My punishment didn't fit the crime.

Months later my friend Stacy was severely disciplined for a minor misdemeanor. Yossi, the branch leader and my supervisor, explained that new missionaries were castigated early to prevent them from making more mistakes. Already brainwashed, I did not even question Stacy's treatment. I had lost my capacity for reflective thought and critical thinking.

We had to be reliable soldiers. Jews for Jesus needed to know that we would take orders and follow directions, especially under pressure.

Occasionally I slipped and was punished. My fine usually consisted of writing extra postcards to donors or contributing money to a Jewish charity such as Trees for Israel. Entire forests were planted from our crimes (partially compensating for the reams of paper used to print tracts).

These penalties were bearable. Other forms of punishment were not. Public humiliation, which usually consisted of chastisement in front of co-workers, and being led to think that I had disappointed God, were particularly painful.

"It hurts to get reprimanded, treated like a fool," I wrote in my dairy after being disciplined. "Yes, the problem is my pride, and I shouldn't care but it still hurts. Does anyone care about me? I feel so alone."

Occasionally rewards were given out. Trips, attractive assignments and raises fell sporadically. A letter of recognition from Moishe or kind word from Yossi could skyrocket my world. But these incidents were rare. I worked hard and took little time off. After serving a year, I would receive one week of vacation. For now I was imprisoned. There would be no reprieve for good behavior. My sentence had begun.

14

If I Believe in Jesus, Why Am I in Hell?

Time zones and travel took their toll. Despite the anxiety, I slept soundly. I would need rest. Training started in the morning.

The prescription for a young missionary was a rigid schedule, little freedom and inadequate rest. For the next several months I would be run like a gerbil on a treadmill. There was no escaping; I adapted.

Day one of training. I reported to Heidi's car at 8:00 a.m. primed for Evangelism 101. Determined to vanquish tardiness, I beat her to the car. She arrived a minute later shouldering a briefcase and an armful of objectives and directives. Half schoolmarm, half warrior, she had her orders and was ready to put me through boot camp.

She drove us to the office. I watched L.A. unfold, marveling at the palm trees which suggested Dr. Suess books. This was my home? The native's were blond, built and spoke Valley Girl vernacular. What was a dark-haired New Yorker doing here?

Sometimes I collided with the unreality of my new life. My B.C. self, a dear friend desperate to wake me from my coma, startled me. "What are you doing in L.A., standing for Jesus and battling Satan?" she'd ask. My true personality, the woman I am today, endangered Ellen the Jew for Jesus. To stay in the group, I suppressed my authentic character. I fought to stay asleep, desperately trying to silence the voices threatening to end my nightmare.

"How did I become a missionary? How did I get saved?" I wrote in my diary. "Someday I'll look back and wonder where the old Ellen went. She died last year on June 2nd. Now I have to rebuild myself and become the woman that God wants me to be."

Yossi assured me that God would use Jews for Jesus to transform me. A good missionary, he explained, must be task oriented, teachable and team oriented. There was no room for self-serving behavior.

The nightmare continued with lesson #1, "How to Get Along with Heidi." Heidi read her notes; I copied the following lecture:

1. If something goes wrong tell Heidi. Do not let Heidi hear it from someone else.

2. It's O.K. to make mistakes. That's how we learn. Do things Heidi's way. Admit it, don't make excuses or try to justify yourself.

3. It's my responsibility to ASK.

4. Ask Heidi not someone else.

5. Erase what you have learned in other branches.

6. Keep perspective on what is real. Tell Heidi the problems you need to deal with.

I listened, accepted, recorded and memorized her words--I underwent mind control. Old thoughts were systematically replaced by new thoughts, old friends by new friends and my old environment by a new one.

What Steven Hassan, a leading exit-counselor and the author of *Combatting Cult Mind Control*, refers to as the four components of mind control were in place. My behavior, thoughts, emotions and access to information were all controlled by Jews for Jesus.

There were no torture chambers, no food deprivation, no

thumb screws or flagellation. I was free to walk about the cordial office filled with sunshine and snacks. The executors of reform were my friends. I trusted them and responded favorably to treatment by passing exams, assimilating material, following directions, and ceasing to think for myself. In the rotting grey matter, dogma spread like bacteria.

All abuse appeared to come from outsiders. Inside the group I felt safe. Beyond the confines of Jews for Jesus, nonbelievers were waiting to crush me (especially my family who, I believed, was controlled by Satan).

Persecution united us. The Worker's Covenant, a document outlining the principles of Jews for Jesus, held us together and controlled our conduct. By signing the covenant, I agreed to follow rules which bound and affected nearly every facet of my life.

"I feel the liberty of the Holy Spirit to enter into this colaboring [sic] relationship with Jews for Jesus, understanding that our purpose is to serve God through the preaching of the Gospel," the document read. "I do so in obedience to the Lord, recognizing that part of my responsibility to God is to do the work of Jews for Jesus."

The precept made separating my relationship with God from my commitment to Jews for Jesus difficult. In my mind, leaving Jews for Jesus was tantamount to leaving God. In addition, the document reinforced the need to obey.

"I agree to accept, in humility, those duties that are assigned by the duly appointed leaders of Jews for Jesus. I agree to accept whatever assignment is made for each term of service with the understanding that reassignments and adjustments in assignment may be made at the discretion of the executive director of Jews for Jesus," the covenant read.

Like parents wishing to raise a child with consistency, Jews for Jesus had me respond to one authority figure, Heidi. I received Heidi's discipline, humbly accepting that correction would further my ministry.

I was particularly vulnerable to mind control because I

desperately wanted to please my supervisors. When I asked Heidi how I was doing, she accused me of fishing for compliments and told me to seek affirmation from God. "You don't deserve praise for just doing your job," she said, reminding me how privileged I was to work for Jews for Jesus. At other times she lavished me with praise and told me how much she loved me.

I told Heidi everything, and she told me what to do. She knew my physical and mental whereabouts, my thoughts, my dreams, my fears. She discovered my weaknesses. She controlled and molded me. She made my life miserable. She was my friend. I feared and loved her.

I was told not to discuss "the work" with anyone else and was assured that friends and co-workers would report me if I disobeyed. "Everyone goes through training," Heidi explained. "The rules are necessary."

Heidi kept me too busy to think. I ran after her like a puppy amazed that someone so short walked so quickly. I followed her on sorties, visits and church meetings. I became a ventriloquist's dummy, repeating the words she fed me and soon mimicked her behavior without strings.

At least in New York and Boston I could talk to others and had some time to myself. Now conversation stopped at Heidi. I had little freedom. Deprived of external information and inner reflection, my mind atrophied.

According to Robert J. Lifton, an expert on mind control and the author of *Thought Reform and the Psychology of Totalism*:

> The most basic feature of the thought reform environment, the psychological current upon which all else depends, is the control of human communication. Through this milieu control [control of a person's surroundings by group practices, isolation from people outside the group, geographical distancing, physical or psychological pressure] the totalist environment seeks

> to establish domain over not only the individual's communication with the outside (all that he sees and hears, reads and writes, experiences, and expresses), but also--in its penetration of his inner life--over what we may speak of as his communication with himself. It creates an atmosphere uncomfortably reminiscent of George Orwell's 1984.

I stopped thinking my own thoughts and lost the ability to make decisions. The group stepped in and made decisions for me. Aside from minor tasks, such as grocery shopping and picking up dry cleaning, Jews for Jesus dictated most of my behavior. They told me how to handle my parents, what to say to contacts, and how to act in church. The little autonomy left reassured me that I was in control of my life.

"We are not a cult, we are not a cult," the other singles and I would joke. After all, we lived alone, were paid, owned cars, dressed nicely, and subsisted on more than brown rice. During campaign training we were even taught how to recognize and deal with cults. I felt sorry for the Moonies and Krishnas I saw on the streets of L.A. We all claimed to know the truth. The truth was we were all under mind control.

Although I didn't live in a communal environment, like most of the Moonies and Krishnas, most of my time was regulated. Heidi chose rest period. I usually napped or ministered to dirty dishes and laundry. I desperately needed to take care of personal matters, but I felt guilty about attending to my affairs. Whether I was trying to relax, pay bills or buy food, I felt I should have been doing evangelism. I wrote in my diary early in April:

> Today I wasn't a missionary. I woke up, figured out my taxes, read the paper, watched T.V., went shopping. My day of rest counted for nothing. It made me see how easily one can get pulled away from what's real, what's eternal. O Lord, don't ever let the

distractions and pleasures of the world overwhelm me.

If guilt wasn't a strong enough governess, Jews for Jesus provided me with standards to regulate my life. The Worker's Covenant dictated codes for appearance, finances, dating, marriage and family life.

I agreed to "avoid questionable forms of amusement," and "notify my supervisor, in writing, of debts incurred in amounts greater than two months' living allowances."

I didn't need relationship guidelines because I almost never dated. I equated dating with the death of my ministry because marriage and ministry were compatible only with a man connected to Jews for Jesus. Fortunately suitors were sparse, so I stayed single. If I had married, leaving the group might have been impossible.

Of course if I wanted to date, the Worker's Covenant provided me with guidelines. I did not need permission to date, but the guidelines read, "dating or courting couples should not entertain one another alone or in their respective places of residence." I was advised to seriously consider the possible consequences of dating a nonstaff person and forbidden to date a nonbeliever.

"Since it is the nature of the ministry to pervade one's whole life, the wise worker will seek a mate who, by temperament and spirituality, is suited to a ministry commitment," the covenant read. "It should not be presumed that courtship and marriage are only personal affairs ... Those planning to stay with the ministry must seek counsel and secure consent of their courtship from those in authority."

While most women my age dated, I resigned myself to a life of loneliness and celibacy. In three years I went on two or three dates--not at all normal behavior for a woman in her mid-twenties. I believed suffering and singleness were the cost of serving God.

"It is a privilege to serve God," I wrote in my journal. "He can use anyone or anything He wants. I relish tomorrow knowing that God may give me an opportunity to change eternity."

Eternity stayed the same--I become depressed. Fatigue, lack of sleep and poor eating habits exacerbated my condition. I blamed the Devil. "The enemy is trying to get to me," I wrote. "I was feeling good about my job, and a few hours later I was feeling lousy. Satan is trying to get his foot in the door so I get discouraged. I won't let him do it. I'll seek God all the harder. I will not be defeated."

My mood swings resembled a cardiogram. One minute I was swinging from Heaven closer to God than Gabriel. The next minute I could be praying for Jesus to return so that I wouldn't have to go on. The changes in temperament were scary and nothing, not even prayer, helped.

"It's hard to know what's real and what's not real," I wrote. "My mood fluctuates so much it's a wonder I haven't driven myself bonkers."

If God loved me so much, why was I so miserable?

15

God Tested Abraham

I settled in L.A.; my family tried adjusting to my exodus. They mourned my departure and kept the memory of my old self alive. The anger, sorrow and stress associated with my situation was killing them.

Six years later, pain remains. As a good journalist, I ask my mother about those years. I attempt objectivity, detachment, but when the interview ends I have only the strength to nap. I feel raw. I feel guilt and know how much she loves me.

My family was my Isaac. I believed that I needed to sacrifice them to prove my love for God. Like Abraham, I laid my family on the alter. The process made my abstract belief concrete.

I never stopped loving my family. I tried to cut them from my mind. Simply functioning in the group was a dilemma; acknowledging my family's pain would have kicked me over the edge. Their love weakened the ministry's influence. The emotional hold had to be loosened.

I could run away, but I couldn't hide. After I moved to L.A., my family found out about my departure. They gathered for a pow wow not sure whether to kill or rescue me. The vote was three to one in favor of strangulation. Bolts of anger struck me from across the country. I had betrayed them.

My parents had produced a monster who preyed on Jews. Bullied and beaten as children for being Jewish, their scars resurfaced.

"Our Jewish history came rushing down on me and rocked me to my very core," my mother explained years later. "The Moonies, Krishnas, Scientology would have been better," she said.

My parents tried to get me to see the destructive nature of my work with Jews for Jesus, but I wouldn't listen. I strained not to think about them. I feared their wrath and wanted to deny the suffering I caused. Heidi, no longer the compassionate person I had pictured over the phone, offered little comfort.

"Heidi, can we write that letter home?" I'd plead.

"We'll get to it," she said, instructing me to finish writing postcards to strangers who supported the ministry.

Finally we composed a note:

Dear Mom & Dad,

I'm writing to let you know that I decided to work for Jews for Jesus. I have moved to Los Angeles. You can write me at ...

I realize that a letter is an inappropriate way to explain my situation. I am very excited about the work I will be doing, and I will tell you more about it once I settle in.

I love you very much. My love for Jesus does not change that.

Love,

Ellen

My coauthors suggested that I write it on a nice card (as if a "nice" picture would deaden the blow). I chose a watercolor of three fish washed up on a pile of rocks, entitled Brown Trout.

The fish emerged, in Boston, a few days later.

Recognizing my handwriting, my mother separated my card from the rest of the mail. She walked to a park to be alone, found a bench along the Charles River, and opened the envelop as if defusing a bomb. She anticipated the worst, but my letter surpassed her expectations.

Instead of being paralyzed by grief, my mother decided to fight. Education, networking, friends and faith sustained her. She would free me and maintain her sanity.

In April my parents attended a Cult Awareness Network conference in Sturbridge, Massachusetts, not sure what to expect. They arrived Friday night and immediately considered leaving.

"We're not like these people," my mother said to my father.

Other parents described crazy behavior. One daughter ate dirt as part of a group ritual. Another consumed only rice. One parent described a son that she hadn't heard from in years.

The next day, opinions changed and illumination began. Speakers enlightened them, and workshops suggested tactics. They met families who understood and supported them. They were not alone.

They met an expert on cults named Louis West who spent time counseling them. He was from L.A. and knew something about Jews for Jesus. The conversation empowered my parents.

"Your daughter loves you very much," he said, after hearing their story and examining some of my letters. "She is a victim."

Victim! The word was a revelation. The label redefined my predicament. Focus shifted. They stopped getting angry at me and concentrated on getting me out of Jews for Jesus. Beneath the miscommunication and the mind control, love resided.

My mother and father supported each other like partners on a see-saw. They read and called and networked and read more. Thought reform, cults, exit-counseling and indoctrination became part of their vocabulary. They learned how to control anger and improve communication.

When I developed the nerve to talk to them they were prepared. I waited until Passover to call. The holiday provided an excuse. I would wish them a happy Passover and get off the phone.

The staff had gathered for a seder; I was among friends. Heidi suggested that I call from the office. Jews for Jesus would pick up the tab. At least I wouldn't have to call collect.

"Do you want me to come in with you?" Heidi asked, as I entered an office.

"I guess so," I said, not sure if I wanted to be alone.

I dialed. My family had probably finished their seder. I wondered who had found the afikomen. My mother answered.

"Hello, Ellen," she said. "Yes, we're all having a nice time. Yes, everyone is here. Sorry you couldn't join us. Thank you for calling."

No one else even wanted to speak to me. I felt abandoned. She hung up. I cried.

16

The Manipulated Learns to Manipulate

Plunging into work drowned my pain. I didn't have much choice. Heidi kept me occupied. I handed out tracts, went on visits, made hundreds of phone calls, and raised funds at churches. I learned about L.A., Jews for Jesus and evangelism. I was too busy to think.

Evangelism always took top priority. The streets of L.A. overflowed with Jesusless souls; our commission was to seek out and enlighten the Jewish ones. We carried our burden twenty-four hours a day. Daily life was our mission field.

How would I establish myself? How would I learn to think like a missionary instead of a petrified neophyte? How would I become a full-time servant of the Lord? I'd adopt the attitude of a missionary. I'd follow Heidi. If I could imitate her I would succeed.

During my first few weeks I fumbled, grappled and groped. I couldn't even Xerox straight. I was trying so hard that I failed constantly.

Reproach struck at all hours. I expected it, but never grew accustomed to or learned how to predict it. In addition, tiny discrepancies could cause eruptions the size of Mount Saint Helens, while major mistakes often received a fleeting comment.

Heidi let me make mistakes, but she didn't tolerate them. Each error furnished an outlet to scold me and strike my pride. In New York I had been special. In Boston allowances were made because I was a volunteer. In L.A. errors would not be accepted.

It never occurred to me to challenge my supervisors. What

right did they have to humiliate and hurt me? I accepted reproof gratefully. The blows would mold me. "You have a tender spirit that bruises easily," my superiors told me. I wanted them to correct this condition.

Morning admonition was the worst. I usually woke early and took an hour to pray, exercise and mentally prepare myself for Hell. In an instant, Heidi could destroy my mood and ruin the rest of the day.

One morning, I was waiting for Heidi to meet me at my apartment. She was late. That was O.K.--she could be late--she was the trainer. I was content writing postcards.

I finished my postcards and started to get a little anxious. Heidi usually wasn't late. Only a little worried, I didn't think of calling her.

The doorbell rang; knocking followed. It was Heidi. I was glad to see her. She was angry. No, more than angry. She was furious.

"What happened to you!" she demanded.

"I was waiting for you," I replied, trying to remain calm and not sound defensive.

"Why didn't you answer the phone?"

"I never heard it ring."

"What do you mean? I've been calling you for the last half hour to let you know I was running late. I asked Lisa and Jeff if they'd seen you. I really thought something had happened to you."

My face turned red. Nervous and scared, I tried not to cry.

"I don't know what happened," I said. "I haven't left my apartment all morning."

She picked up the phone and called Lisa. The phone worked. Heidi spoke to Lisa, hung up and handed me the phone. The grey ringer button was switched to OFF.

"How could you be so careless?" she asked. "This can't continue. Don't you know I need to depend on you?"

I said nothing. Trying to explain would have made matters worse.

I aspired to be like this woman? I emulated her. I dreamed of being "super missionary" just like her. Everyone on staff told me I was blessed to be working with the best. I believed them.

Heidi was a master at handling me and her contacts (the people we "ministered" to). She'd slide into their lives, identify why they refused to accept Jesus and try to turn them into believers. I would duplicate her efforts. I would learn how to manipulate people too.

Most of the manipulation took place on visits. Visits were the meat of our ministry. We lived for the one on one confrontations and prayed for conversions. A large part of training was learning the dynamics of these encounters.

We called the visits "interviews." There were in-person interviews, phone visits, drop-ins, and bird-dog visits (arranged by another believer). The initial interview served to qualify contacts and provide opportunities for witnessing. Like chiropractors building a practice, we needed a constant stream of clients.

Each contact was labeled and filed away. Last name first, first name last, address, phone number, date, and origin of the contact all went on an index card. "Saved" people got blue cards; those heading to Hell got yellow. I always hesitated changing cards after a conversion; I could never be sure that the commitment would stick, and I hated losing UJ (unbelieving Jew) contacts because finding Jewish people to witness to was difficult.

People were categorized as lonely, angry, hostile, selling (trying to get me to buy something else), open or curious. Usually people who were hostile or selling were not visited very often. Lonely people were shown how God could meet their needs. Angry people were encouraged to uncover the roots of their hostility. Curious people were pushed into being open, and open people were pushed into believing in Jesus.

During my first months of training I accompanied Heidi on at least six UJ and two JB (Jewish believer) visits each week.

I said little and noted Heidi's tone of voice, body language and mannerisms. Watching Heidi was fascinating. She hacked away at belief systems using the Christian Bible like a Samurai with a sword.

I learned how to plan and prepare for visits, how to set goals, use Scripture, challenge a contact, cultivate other contacts, and follow up on visits. There was a list of procedures to obey. Adhering to them was imperative. These were God's rules. Most contacts thought that we were just paying a friendly visit, but we had a mission to preach Jesus.

A large percentage of the people we saw were elderly. Elders were an obvious target because they were easy to influence, often home, plentiful and lonely. They'd tolerate my harangue in exchange for an hour of companionship--many had no other visitors.

Sometimes I went door to door in nursing homes. No one ever stopped me. The authorities probably thought I was someone's granddaughter; they were happy to have someone visit.

Before entering a room, I'd check the door for a name. "Hi Mrs.______ [Stein, Goldsmith, Abramowitz], my name's Ellen," I'd say. "Sometimes I visit people here. I was wondering if you'd like a little company?"

The residents usually accepted my invitation. On the first visit they did most of talking. They discussed their children, their illness, their dead spouse. I'd steer the conversation to spiritual matters. "What do you think about God? How were you brought up? Conservative, Reform, Orthodox?" Like a skilled talk show host, I'd warm them up and unleash my true agenda.

"What do you think about the Messiah?" I'd ask. "What would you think if I told you I thought Jesus was the Mashiach?"

Usually this startled them, but I knew not to push too far; I wanted to secure another visit.

One of my first visits with Heidi was to see a woman

named Sarah. She was very sick and had just returned from the hospital armed with an arsenal of pills. In her condition, I'm surprised she even let us in.

We parked in front of her house and paused to discuss tactics and pray. "Jesus, please open Sarah's heart," Heidi pleaded.

Heidi and I got out of the car, walked to the front door and rang the bell. Sarah's husband Sid answered the door. A pair of bouncing, barking poodles, and the fragrance of fried fish and pet food greeted us. I held my nose and tried to dodge the poodles who were starting to snarl.

Sarah showed us seats and the conversation started.

"How was the hospital?" Heidi asked, enunciating every word so that Sarah, who was hard of hearing, would understand.

"Oh, my sons are fine," Sarah replied.

"No, I said how was your stay at the hospital?"

"Oh, I'm very sick. The doctors keep giving me medicine, but nothing seems to help."

"God wants to help you," Heidi said.

"I know about God. I've prayed, but I still feel sick."

"Sarah," Heidi said, moving closer, trying to capture the old woman's attention. "Jesus wants to help you so you will never be sick again."

"Please, I don't want to hear about Jesus again," Sarah said.

"Sarah, remember what I have been telling you about God and Jesus?" Heidi asked.

"Yes, I know what you have said."

"Have you thought about asking Jesus for help?"

"No, Jesus is not for me," she said. "I have my God."

"But Jesus is the only way for you to get better," Heidi said, picking up her Christian Bible and reading a story about how Jesus healed people at Gennesaret.

"Jesus can heal your body, but more important he wants

to forgive you so you can go to Heaven."

Sarah squirmed in her seat and looked away. She didn't want to hear any more.

"I'm feeling nauseated," she said. "I've asked God to take away my dizziness, but nothing has happened. I feel so sick sometimes I just want to die."

"Maybe God is keeping you here for a reason," Heidi said. "Maybe God is giving you a chance to accept Jesus."

We left with Heidi's questions and poodle barks ringing in the air. I don't remember seeing her again. She was too closed to justify another visit even though she would have benefited from a friendly call. But we were commissioned to convert not comfort. We moved on.

Although we preached to all of our contacts, there were some people we liked more than others. I tolerated UJ's who served stale cake and coffee resembling witches brew. I listened to widows repeat, "What you need is a nice Jewish boy," like a mantra and suffered through lectures entitled, "Why You Should See the Rabbi." Jesus loved them; I'd endure them.

Jan was not one of these cases; Heidi and I quickly grew fond of her. A Gentile believer, from a church which Heidi attended, passed on Jan's name. The first visit was only a phone call away. Heidi spoke with Jan and made a date to meet at Denny's Restaurant.

When we arrived at the restaurant, Jan was already there. Heidi and I ordered coffee; Jan stuffed her incredibly cute kid with French fries.

Heidi treated Jan very differently than she had Sarah. She admired Jan's outfit and remarked at how adorable her son was. Since this was a contact visit, Jan did 90% of the talking. Heidi's agenda was simple; she wanted to qualify Jan to see how interested she was in Jesus. If Jan was open, Heidi would propose a Bible study.

The plan worked and within weeks the three of us were engaged in a study. The situation was a great learning experience for me. Heidi made the operation look easy. She lead Jan through *Y'shua* (a book of prophecies written by Moishe Rosen). Jan accepted most of what Heidi showed her in the Christian Bible. Her life was difficult. She was a single, unemployed mom, living with two kids in a housing project.

Jan was looking for help. What she needed was a secure job and day care. What she wanted was a terrific guy to marry, love and provide for her and her children. These real solutions would take work. In the interim Jesus would do. But would Jesus really solve her dilemmas?

17

A Branch Is More Than Part of a Tree

I was a professional missionary. Evangelism was my livelihood. Friends from college struggled in law school, learned to teach elementary math and analyzed junk bonds. I preached the Gospel. They had lovers, friends, husbands and wives; I had the L.A. branch. The branch was home, the residents family.

Purpose and abuse united us; the branch sustained us.
The branch was more than an office. It was the foundation for activity. Our us-against-the-world mentality required support.

A branch was defined as: a network of operations in a greater metropolitan area that contains a Jewish population of at least 100,000 in which the evangelistic activities of Jews for Jesus are carried out on a daily basis.

The purpose of the branch was to proclaim the Gospel and propagate an image that Jews believed in Jesus. Providing space for fellowship, teaching and service was another priority. We wanted to break ground and make waves. Simultaneously we hoped to show how normal, how educated, how sweet, how typically Jewish we were.

When I worked for Jews for Jesus, branches existed in New York, Boston, Chicago, San Francisco, Los Angeles and Toronto. Jewish populations in Israel, England, Russia, and South Africa have also been tapped.

Several of my former co-workers, I believe, are now in Russia trying to convert Jews. Russian Jews, both at home and abroad, are especially vulnerable because they lack Jewish education and hunger for spirituality.

Since setting up a branch abroad was difficult, especially

in countries like Israel which oppose Christian missions targeting Jews, Jews for Jesus trained foreigners and sent them back to their native countries. The world-wide outreach enhanced the ministry's image.

The L.A. branch, where much of the training took place, was located in the San Fernando Valley. The words "Jews for Jesus," painted on the second story office window, proclaimed our existence. A score of mini-vans with "Jews for Jesus" painted on the sides helped spread our message. People may not have had the pleasure of meeting us, but they knew we existed.

Despite our name and the nature of our work, the office functioned like a business. Filing, typing, sorting mail and answering the phones were all routine. UPS visited us just like the pizza place and nail salon down the street.

We did more than deliver pizza and give manicures, however; we fought for God. The office was our point of entry and departure. The building served as arsenal (storage place for tracts and books), training ground and strategic outpost. Several times a week we met there to defend ourselves with prayer.

Assaults and insults were familiar events. Many Jewish people hated us. Prank phone calls and spray paint violated the office. Strangers shouted, yelled and spit on us. Cigarettes singed my flesh and umbrellas stabbed my body. Stupid and fearless, I stood my ground, praised the Lord and kept witnessing. The opposition could kill me; they'd go to jail, I'd go to Heaven and Jesus would be glorified, I thought.

"To say that rabbis and Jewish community leaders don't endorse our work for God would be an understatement," says a Jews for Jesus promotional pamphlet. "In a sense, this opposition is a tribute to our effectiveness ... However, Christian leaders who endorse us draw much fire from Jewish leaders and so very few do," the brochure says. "For this reason, we have had to take much of the fire directly."

Many of the people who did support Jews for Jesus

viewed us as the Green Berets of Evangelism. Some had never met a Jewish person and loved hearing how we came to believe in Jesus. A careful image was constructed to win support. We wanted people to think of us as evangelistic, creative, courageous, mobile, versatile, honest, consistent and broad-based.

Evangelical Christians were encouraged to use Jews for Jesus as an educational resource and send money to fund the ministry and the names of Jewish friends for us to witness to. We told the congregants to tithe (donate money, usually 10% of income) to their church first. Reinforcing the importance of donating to the church first helped Jews for Jesus maintain good church relations. Supporters received more requests for money and a newsletter filled with battle stories, designed to inspire and elicit donations.

We were proud of our reputation and aggressive stance and often fought harder after an assault. The inspiration for the Y'shua campaign, a multi-million dollar scheme to advertise Jesus, was sparked by a splattering of graffiti. After the incident, staff members began to pray, and someone came up with the idea to lift Jesus by publicizing his name in national magazines and newspapers.

Every knock was a boost. I remember listening to a radio show featuring Yossi, our branch leader, and someone from the Jewish community. We had clearly lost the debate, but Yossi would not admit defeat.

"Why are your tails between your legs?" he asked the next day. "We won."

Our motto was: sticks and stones may break my bones, but Jesus is still the Messiah. God was on our side, and He was bigger than any adversary.

Co-laborers, people who helped coordinate behind-the-scenes work, were our back-up troops. They watered us with encouragement, loaded our tract bags, accompanied us on sorties, stuffed envelops and greeted guests at Bible study. Their warmth and support often helped me through a week.

Missionaries were expected to recruit, develop and manage volunteers. Volunteers were a source of labor and new staff workers.

Jews for Jesus looked for enthusiastic Jewish believers to bring on staff. We were asked to send the names, addresses and phone numbers of potential workers.

"The only requirements are that they are Jewish, they love the Lord and they are interested in sharing their faith," a memo from the director of recruiting said. "Don't worry whether or not they are a doctor, or a lawyer, housewife or even if they are a relatively new believer."

Many staff members started as volunteers. Gradually they became more involved. Commitment escalated until they were on staff. I started distributing a few tracts and a year later I was handing out thousands. For the first three years of service our contract lasted for a year. After the fourth year a three year commitment began. The longer you stayed the harder it was to leave.

We were an odd bunch. A handful of renegades out to take L.A. for the Lord. During training I read a book called *Rules for Radicals*, which described ways to create mass organizations, seize power and change society. Several of the senior staff members had been hippies smoking dope on the streets of San Francisco in the sixties. The spirit of the era lingered, ironically channeled into rigid, narrow-minded, Fundamentalist Christianity.

I thought we were on the cutting edge of evangelism. I felt revolutionary, electric, dynamic. In reality I was two steps away from being a nun. I didn't dress in black or wear a habit, but I agreed to "dress and conduct myself in a demeanor that is honoring to the Lord and in modest good taste [and] avoid questionable forms of amusement." If I had any doubt as to the propriety of a given activity, I consulted my supervisor.

Each Monday staff gathered for breakfast, prayer and announcements. A different missionary hosted every week.

During my first few months of work I learned to keep quiet during these breakfasts. Too many words could result in humiliation. It was not my place to talk to everyone about everything. I learned to listen.

Announcements, during these meetings, were often routine: "Designate a specific place when addressing correspondence to HQ; order materials through the computer; do not leave things around the office; logs are due at staff breakfast," Yossi would tell us.

Sometimes we discussed serious issues. Two weeks after my arrival Jim and Tammy Bakker hit the press. The incident was an embarrassment to the entire Christian community. Air-conditioned dog houses and infidelity were a lousy testimony. We were told not to deal with the issue. "It's not the individuals who matter it's Jesus," I was instructed to say to nonbelievers who brought up the Bakkers.

After announcements the host or hostess offered a devotional. Suffering was a popular theme. Everybody who was anybody suffered in the Scriptures. Abraham, Joseph, the prophets, David and Paul lived for Murphy's Law. It's by our brokenness and suffering that we can relate to God, I was told.

Prayer came next. Since we were usually suffering there was plenty to pray about. Each co-worker would state a few requests; we would shut our eyes and pray out loud for each other. Sometimes the requests were material: a new car, help with finances or the right apartment. Sometimes spiritual: salvation for a UJ or new people to minister to.

Monday morning ended with writers cramp. We wrote postcards to our donors:

Dear ________

Shalom to you in ______. I'm writing to thank you for your recent gift to Jews for Jesus. Your contribution to the ministry `and partnership since 19__ means so much to me as I serve in L.A. I am a new missionary here. Please pray that God will __________.`

I wrote sixty postcards a week. As punishment, sometimes I wrote more.

By the time the postcard writing session was over, many of us were ready for a sortie. We'd drive to the office, pick up tracts and head to LAX Airport, Westwood Village, downtown L.A. or a college campus.

L.A. was a tough place to distribute tracts. "Nobody walks in L.A." Finding street traffic was rough. Even good spots dried up if we visited them too often.

We tried to be creative and discover new places and ways to hold sorties. I handed out broadsides in Beverly Hills, on Ventura Boulevard and before the Academy Awards. Rock concerts, baseball games, even the zoo became territory to win for the Lord.

Mother's Day, Valentines Day, New Years and the Fourth of July all provided sortie themes. When a holiday wasn't handy, we concocted an event. We'd paint signs, dress-up and write chants to promote our message. On Cripple Day we bandaged up our limbs, grabbed crutches and hobbled about UCLA. On Ugly Day staff members dressed like hobos and buffoons. During Valentine's Day we handed out tracts and chanted, "Be smart; don't be stupid; trust in Jesus, not in Cupid."

Yossi had a flair for performance. A born, Born Again stand-up comic, he was a fool for Christ. He interviewed himself using a banana as a microphone and made fun of his looks.

I played the vacuous Valley Girl. I'd raise my voice an octave, repeat "like" after every other word, and pretend to be interested in shoes, shopping and manicures. Sometimes we drew a small crowd. The curious onlookers often asked about our message.

We thought God was using our foolishness to win souls for Christ. We envisioned the walls of Hell crashing down about us and believed we were winning L.A. for the Lord.

18

Manna from Ma Bell

There were over half a million Jewish people in L.A.; surely some wanted to hear about Jesus. But sharing the Gospel with Jewish people often felt like selling bear traps to PETA (People for the Ethical Treatment of Animals).

Heidi assured me that God would provide. I wasn't so sure. Obviously her faith was stronger than mine. I doubted myself, my training and God. After a few months of instruction, Heidi was cutting me loose. My weekly goals would include two solo UJ visits. Eventually I would need 80-100 people to minister to. How would I get contacts?

Heidi urged me to pray for a burden for the lost (concern for people who didn't embrace Jesus). I prayed. I envisioned souls in Hell. I asked others to pray for me. I remained more concerned with meeting goals than saving souls.

Heidi lectured on how to build a caseload. Contacts could come from anywhere: training, spiritual life, friends. Fear of rejection, laziness and frustration could jeopardize my effort. Being available for ministry and trusting God were key ingredients to increase a caseload.

Heidi had all the answers. I listened, but contacts didn't fall from the sky like manna. They grew from routine tasks, hard work, creativity and initiative. Bird Dogs (believers who pointed to contacts), Jewish clubs and businesses, Bible studies, interfaith marriages and sorties were all sources.

My savior was Ma Bell. Within a few hours of calling I realized that the contacts I needed were only seven digits away. With the phone I could reach out and touch hundreds of people. Approaching people over the phone was easy and economical. In seconds I could dial and talk to a UJ from the safety of my apartment. If they yelled, I distanced myself from the receiver or hung up.

A seasoned salesperson, I adapted cold calling techniques to evangelism. The phone company even provided me with a list of potential UJ's. I let my fingers walk through the white pages from Aaron to Goldberg, Horowitz to Zwetchkenbaum. I covered the newsprint with marks, noting names to consider calling, names to call back, and names never to call again.

Telemarketing Jesus usually began at 7:00 p.m. I joined the ranks of college fund raisers, moonlighters selling magazines, and legislators seeking re-election. My purpose was to inform people that Jews can and should believe in Jesus. My goals were to build my caseload, add names to a mailing list, witness and get visits. Winning trust took weeks, but with persistence people often considered meeting with me.

My approach was simple. I pretended to conduct a survey. I asked three questions: (1) Have you ever heard of Jews for Jesus? (2) What do you think of the idea that some Jewish people think that Jesus is the Jewish Messiah? (3) What do you think about Jesus? The open ended questions left room for discussion.

Cold calls were my bucking bronco: I rode conversations for minutes without falling off. I could diffuse an angry UJ or spark curiosity. By revealing things about myself and never entirely answering questions, I left opportunity for future contact. People always responded. Some slammed the phone, or swore and slammed the phone. Many stayed on the line. I spoke with angry Holocaust survivors, lonely shut-ins and curious housewives. I visualized the person on the other end; I listened and sounded caring. I scored visits. My experience on Seventh Avenue selling sportswear had not been useless.

Cold calling built my caseload and my ego. I received a memo from Yossi commending me on my activities:

Dear Ellen:

I've noticed that over the last few weeks your statistics for UJ calling have been impressively high. This includes not only the number of attempts, but the number of completed calls. I wanted to commend you for doing a fine job, Ellen. I understand you also went on five first time UJ visits last week with contacts you generated from cold UJ calling. Again, good work.

May He continue to use you for the advance of His Kingdom, and may He bless you abundantly as you serve and live for Him.

In Y'shua,

Yossi

The encouragement was all I needed to dig into the G's and H's in the phone book. I was determined to win souls for the Lord. But the more I did, the more my goals increased, and the harder I worked.

First time visits were a treat. After speaking over the phone for weeks, I grew eager to meet contacts, and they wanted to see me. I sounded so nice over the phone. "What would a Jew for Jesus look like? How can she be a Jew for Jesus--she sounds so nice?" they were thinking.

Contact visits resembled blind dates. (Once a contact actually said, "I'll be the one with the rose.") We'd set a time and meeting place and describe each other. I always had a few restaurants in mind. Often I offered to drop by their home.

Before the date, I dressed nicely and become nervous. I prayed that they would like me and my message. Sometimes we clicked and sometimes we didn't. Regardless of the chemistry, I always desired a second date and wanted to meet the family. I usually ended a relationship only when a contact died.

Many of my contacts were interesting people. Living in L.A., I periodically met people associated with Hollywood.

Gloria, one of my favorite contacts, worked for Fox

studios. Initially I called her for months without scoring a visit. One evening, during a phone conversation, she asked me if I'd like to stop by for lunch. My calender was out before she finished her thought, and we made a date.

The following week I drove out to the Fox studio. Gloria left my name at the entrance, and I sailed through the gate past movie sets and screening rooms. I parked and walked over to Gloria's trailer. The receptionist pointed her out, and I introduced myself. She looked more glamorous than I had imagined. Her clothing was impeccable, her hair elegant and her nails long and polished. I felt a little dowdy. Fortunately, she was as amiable in person as she had been over the phone.

We walked over to the employee "cafeteria." I was expecting simple self-serve fair. The establishment was elegant, the food excellent and the atmosphere electric. I tried to ignore the ambience in order to focus on my visit. But the things of the world obviously still had a hold.

Gloria told me about her life. I already new a great deal from our telephone conversations. She had several children and lived by herself in Hollywood. Travel was her passion. Every time I visited her she was either planning or recovering from a cruise.

I asked her about her belief in God and her Jewish upbringing. Although she was raised Conservative, she rarely went to services; but she did believe in God. I tried to relate to her by sharing my background. I explained how I had left the glamorous world of retailing for Jesus and tried to get her to think about the Gospel. She'd listen, but she was only curious, not open.

"That's fine for you," was her usual response.

"No, Gloria, Jesus is for you too," I'd say.

On Saturday, I sometimes visited a woman named Bev who also had connections to show business. I called her one night while perusing the C's. Like Gloria, she was happy to have me visit, but she wasn't about to accept Jesus.

"I'd rather go to Hell than follow Jesus," she told me.

I continued visiting Bev despite her hatred for Jesus. I

prayed for her salvation and asked others to pray for her. I even asked if I could pray for her employment. I prayed and her work situation improved.

Although Bev remained an unbeliever, our relationship developed. She told me about her trips to Vegas, showed me pictures of grandchildren, and gave me fresh lemons from a tree on the patio. I continued to tell her about Jesus.

Although contacts like Gloria and Bev liked seeing me, I couldn't visit them very often because they weren't open to my message. On holidays I sent greeting cards. I invited them to Jews for Jesus events and called every few weeks to see if God was moving in their lives, but nothing changed. I prayed for their salvation and for new, open contacts. Their cards went into my cold file and I continued to work through the phone book.

19

Souls or Stats?

What an awful feeling it was to be driving along the 405 with a cup of cold coffee, a pile of caseload cards, and an empty calender with visit requirements to meet. Even the Hollywood Hills and California sunshine couldn't lift my spirits.

The drive to save souls and make goals was constant. The moment I met my target the requirements were raised. Sometimes the pressure came from headquarters; sometimes directly from my supervisor in the form of memorandums.

Dear Ellen:

You're doing a fine job at consistently hitting your present interview goals. I'd like you to "up the ante," now. Make your minimum goal 10 visits with the majority being UJ visits. As I said, let that be your minimum goal, but strive for more. In time, you should be consistently hitting between 12 and 14 visits a week.

The memo, from Yossi, sent shock waves through my psyche. Where would I find twelve to fourteen UJs a week to meet with?

"I've been feeling tired and burnt because people are so closed," I wrote in my journal. "I feel like I have nothing to say to them."

Even taking time off was stressful. I couldn't relax when goals weren't met. Occasionally during a particularly successful week I was able to take a break, but then I'd think "I should be doing evangelism." At best I allowed myself to enjoy the ocean following a beach sortie or shopping after a visit in a mall.

After a day of searching for UJs, Stacy, Jeff (two other single missionaries) and I would unite over dinner and complaints.

"I don't know how I'm going to make my goals this week," we'd cry, griping about "the work" and our ministry. Feeling guilty about complaining, we'd joke and draw A's in the air to symbolize our poor Attitude.

"I need to change my attitude towards the ministry and repent for resentment and bitterness," I scribbled again and again in my journal like a punished child forced to write, "I will not disrupt class."

Commiserating with Jeff and Stacy didn't help. I felt there was no outlet; no way to improve our predicament. Once a year I had an opportunity to discuss problems with an ombudsman, who was part of Jews for Jesus Board of Directors, but I was conditioned to uphold the ministry and so did not voice my complaints. I tried to convince myself that I was blessed to be doing God's work with such an illustrious organization.

Pressure worsened as the week progressed. Most people look forward to Saturday night; I often dreaded it. What if I didn't fulfil my duties? What would happen? How would I explain the numbers on my work log? Would I be allowed to continue missionary work? My fears were irrational. I almost always met or surpassed my goals, and if the totals were scanty I didn't get in trouble. But I didn't want to disappoint myself, my supervisors and God.

To compound matters, sometimes I competed with and snapped at Stacy (obviously Christ hadn't completely transformed my character). We were friends, but we were also rivals vying for UJs. When Lisa and Heidi departed, we were left to split most of the remaining female contacts. (All of my contacts, with the exception of a few older men, were female. Showing interest in a man when I was only interested in introducing him to Jesus was discouraged.)

Stacy joined staff after me and initially had some trouble establishing herself. I should have been more supportive. A generous missionary would have offered to give her a few contacts. Instead I fought.

There were moments when I hated Stacy and times when I couldn't contain the stress; the slightest incident ignited me. Stacy and I often discussed our contacts, trying to keep a lid on jealousy.

One particularly terrible week Stacy told me about a new contact she was going to visit. The UJ was related to one of my JBs! The JB had mentioned her dying aunt to Stacy, and Stacy had happily copied down the information. Now she had a first visit with a contact who was rightfully mine.

As a true Christian, my spirit should have been centered on poor lost souls. I should not have been concerned with who got the visits. Forget salvation; I wanted contacts. I prayed for God to change my heart; I asked Him to give me a burden for the lost. I concocted effigies of people in Hell. I remained desperate for contacts.

Each Friday night my trained eye scanned the Bible study for new faces. It was my responsibility to know the name, rank (UJ, JB, GB, UG), and hopefully get the phone number of everyone who attended the service.

Yossi wrote to me:

I want to remind you that when it comes to handling the attendance book on Friday nights, you'll want to treat this as an opportunity to get to know as many people as possible. This way, we'll be able to identify and qualify them enabling us to have a more accurate account for the weekly report as to the breakdown.

I'd greet strangers with a smile (just as I had been greeted initially in New York).

"Hi, my name's Ellen," I would say. "How'd you hear

about services?"

Some people were brought by friends, others received broadsides, a few came at our invitation. A short dialogue usually followed.

"So what do you think about Jesus?" I'd ask as if discussing the weather.

Within a few minutes I usually had my information and ended the conversation.

Names entered a book along with a two-letter designation. UJ's received special treatment. If the UJ was a woman I sprang into action, cornered her, became extra friendly and tried to schedule a visit. When a UJ was male I'd alert one of the male missionaries. "Hey, Jeff, see that man with the glasses and the plaid shirt? He's a hot UJ," I'd say.

Friday night Bible study was an important component of our ministry. The meetings provided a place for Jewish believers to congregate and reinforce their identity. The gatherings were also an excellent arena for witnessing. Evangelistic sermons were common and sometimes included an opportunity for UJs to pray to receive Jesus.

Services differed between branches, but they all had the familiar Jewish flavor. The festivities began with singing and a word of greeting. Most of the music was upbeat and sounded Semitic. Candle lighting, announcements and a Christian Bible lesson followed. A blessing over bread and wine signaled the close of services, and everyone was invited to enjoy refreshments.

While guests munched on cheese & crackers, we ministered to congregations and set up visits. I knew the importance of these meetings. A Friday night study had been my first exposure to the group. If I hadn't felt so comfortable and welcome I would not have returned. Perhaps I would not have joined Jews for Jesus.

20

Jock for Jesus

In the eighties, like many people my age, I was part of the fitness boom. I ground my Reeboks into the gym floor, suffered through killer aerobics, lifted weights and road exercycles nowhere. When I became a believer, my priorities shifted. Having a great body was no longer important, but maintaining my health was. Exercise was one of the few activities that I made time for.

Working out was a way of life in L.A. I decided to join the trend. I bought a trial membership at the Sports Connection. The club had two dance studios, free weights, Nautilus, massage, a snack bar, a sauna, and dozens of UJs.

Sometimes I'd strike up a conversation about Jesus between sets of shoulder presses or sit-ups. When I wore a Jews for Jesus T-shirt, people sometimes approached me.

"Jews for Jesus? I've always wanted to know what that was about," they'd ask.

People felt more comfortable relating to me in the gym. I guess I looked more normal straining under a barbell than standing on a street corner. Sweat was a great equalizer.

I acquired several contacts at the gym and even held a few visits there. "I can't talk now," I'd say, gasping for breath in the middle of an aerobics class. "But I'd be happy to talk to you after we finish." When our heart-rates returned to normal, I'd suggest talking over fruit juice or Gatorade.

The club was a great place to schedule visits because people felt comfortable there. I never would have scored a visit with Blanche without the club. Blanche and I first met at the Santa Monica Farmer's Market. She was shopping; I was trying to pick up a few UJs and get rid of my tracts. Blanche was so angry when she saw me that she nearly dropped her produce. She ripped up a tract and tried to grab more. When that failed to work, she began to yell at me.

"You traitor!" she cried. "Do your parents know what you are doing? Shame on you!"

Her actions were nothing new. I was used to the harassment. I expected it. Opposition meant that I was doing my job. Jewish people were noticing me and getting angry. I believed Satan was upset and that he was sending people to bother me.

I let her defuse.

"Why are you so upset?" I asked, hoping to engage her in conversation.

"I don't know when I've been this angry."

"What is making you so angry?"

"Do you know what this is?" she asked, baring her arm to reveal a five digit tattoo.

For a moment I remained silent, unsure how to respond to the Holocaust survivor and address my own distress.

"Yes, I know what that is," I said, trying to remain calm.

"This is what Jesus has done for me."

"What happened to you is terrible, but it has nothing to do with Jesus. Jesus came to end the suffering that you went through."

"You're meshugge" she said, but now she was calmer.

We talked for a few more minutes. Miraculously, Blanche actually gave me her phone number. I promised to send her some more information and call in a few weeks.

"Maybe we can get together sometime and discuss the issue," I suggested and went back to handing out tracts.

I mailed Blanche some material and a nice letter. She thanked me for the packet, but said she wasn't interested in learning more. I was disappointed but not surprised.

I called Blanche several times a month and sent her cards during Jewish holidays. We became friendlier and Blanche expressed a desire to meet with me. Through the course of our conversations we established that we both attended The Sports Connection and so made arrangements to meet there.

An hour before the visit I dissolved my fears in jazzercize

class. When I got to the locker room Blanche was there waiting for me. We made ourselves comfortable on a pair of chaise lounges and started to talk. I tried to warm Blanche up by talking about my family. She listened attentively, but when I switched topics to Jesus she stiffened. She didn't want to hear any more.

Meanwhile a band of UJ's, overhearing the conversation, had gathered around us. They were all on Blanche's side and leapt to defend her. I was clearly outnumbered, but they were dressed only in towels and appeared harmless. I took them all on, managing to state the Gospel despite their fuming. After the battle I cooled off in the steam room.

21

Gefilte Fishing

The supermarket was an excellent place to shop for contacts. Among the jars of gefilte fish and boxes of matzah I often found a fine selection of UJ's. Health food stores and Jewish specialty food shops were especially fruitful places to do business. Many of the organic food gurus I met buying bulk tofu were Jewish as were most of the customers purchasing kosher chickens and knishes.

California supermarkets were often open around the clock, so I struck at all hours. Sometimes my approach was subtle. Noticing a box of Passover cake mix in a cart, I'd query the owner about the merits of the mix. In a few minutes, if I was lucky, we'd been in a heated discussion about the challenge of baking without leaven and flour. We'd exchange tips and recipes, and I would hint at the nature of my spirituality. "I'm Jewish," I'd explain, "But I believe Jesus is the Messiah."

After warming up to me, through the discussion of baking techniques, coldly dismissing me was hard. Usually dialogue ended with a polite, "I need to get back to my shopping," or "It's been nice talking with you." Occasionally conversation concluded with hostility or a sincere desire to hear more about my faith. I always carried paper to record names and a small bundle of literature to offer information.

The direct approach to picking-up contacts involved wearing a Jews for Jesus T-shirt into the store. Instantly I became a billboard for the Lord. My favorite shirt proclaimed, "Jesus Made Me Kosher." Usually someone near me in the check-out line would ask what the statement meant. I'd explain that I believed Jesus had made me kosher--clean in God's eyes.

I discovered many other ways to connect with Jewish people. There was the post office, my apartment complex and the mall. Once I went Israeli folk dancing; another day I attended synagogue services. Heidi suggested reeling in contacts at the car wash, but people usually were preoccupied with their vehicles.

My apartment was a perfect front for missionary work. Initially I concealed my calling. I wanted my neighbors to get to know me before they learned about my vocation. There would be plenty of time for witnessing.

One afternoon, I forgot to cover up my "Jesus Made Me Kosher" T-shirt, and the word was out: I was a Jew for Jesus. The news spread through the complex. Some of my neighbors didn't care. Others were outraged. One woman, realizing that she couldn't have me evicted, was especially nasty to me. Each time she saw me she commented on what Christians had done to hurt the Jews and reminded me that I was contributing to the destruction of her people.

Many of the other women in the complex grew to like me despite my beliefs. We'd share afternoons by the pool and have intimate discussions about our families. I welcomed the break from proselytizing.

Ruth, the woman who lived below my apartment, treated me like a granddaughter. She always asked how I was and invited me to visit anytime except when "Jeopardy" was on T.V. Her children, grandchildren and great grandchildren were always dropping by, and I managed to meet and witness to many of them. I established a friendship with one of her granddaughters. After winning her trust I convinced her to study the Bible with me.

Most of the people that I successfully converted were first introduced to me by other people on my caseload. Heidi taught me to always cultivate contacts for more contacts and I heeded her advice.

Ruth's granddaughter was one example. Judy, a friend of one of my JB's, was another. Arranging a meeting with Judy was tough. She didn't showed up for our first date, and she canceled the second and third. I was ready to give up, but Judy's friend insisted that she was open and really wanted to hear about Jesus.

I decided to drop in on Judy the next time I was in the area. My plan worked. Judy was home and invited me into her house, but Judy was not open and didn't seem to want to hear about Jesus. She said that I could visit again, so I made a note to follow up a few weeks later.

Martha, her friend, was disappointed.

"I don't think she's as open as you thought," I told her.

"I've known her for about six months and she's asked a lot of questions about my faith," Martha said. "Can't you give it another try?"

"O.K.," I said. "I won't give up."

Together we prayed for Judy's salvation, and I made plans to visit Judy again. The next visit took place as scheduled. The encounter was very different than our first meeting. Judy bombarded me with questions about Jesus, and decided to become a follower herself. Surprised and elated, I happily lead her in the sinner's prayer.

Within weeks Judy started attending church. Her daughter quickly became a believer too, but her husband resisted following Jesus. His stance pained Judy and threatened their marriage. Judy didn't know what to do. Witnessing to family members was hard, so like many other Jewish believers Judy turned to us to turn the screws. Yossi came to the rescue. The operation took several months, but Yossi successfully chipped away Art's resistance until he became a believer too.

I'm baptized at night in the Atlantic ocean at Brighton Beach.

A group of New York campaigners. Moishe Rosen, director of Jews for Jesus, is in the first row on the right. To find me: start with the woman sitting to the left of Moishe (in the first row), then count two heads directly in back of her.

Jews for Jesus advertisement in the December 7, 1987 issue of *Newsweek* magazine.

22

Campaign

Think back to your favorite vacation: a trip to Europe, a ten day cruise, a back-packing expedition. How would you feel about an all expense paid trip to New York City? Tour the entire town. See the Empire State Building, the subway holes, Macy's, more subway holes, South Street Sea Port, yet more subway holes. Distribute literature, witness, perform street drama, reach Jews, win college credit and points in Heaven. This is not vacation--this is Summer Campaign.

Vacation benefits were not one of the ministry's strong points. After a year of service, I was entitled to one week off. But that was O.K. Jews for Jesus was sending me on campaign, and I was as thrilled as a child off to summer camp.

"The next six weeks are going to be an adventure with God," I wrote in my journal. "Who knows what He has planned and how each of us will be used for His glory. It's exciting to be part of it."

Two weeks of training, four weeks of constant ministry and no goals (scheduling visits, cultivating contacts, number of tracts, etc.). Nothing to think about but sorties. I couldn't wait to leave L.A. I'd see old friends, visit familiar haunts and hand out thousands of tracts. Manhattan was one of the richest Jewish mission fields in the world. I was determined to reach a few of them.

Preparing for the trip was a cinch. I threw all my Jews for Jesus T-shirts, several pair of jeans, and some sneakers in a bag. In our evangelistic army the troops dressed identically. The sameness created the illusion that we campaigners were a massive army. A few dresses and skirts were included, among the sweat socks, for training classes and church.

Before leaving for the "Promised Land," I carefully copied

my contact cards. A brief note from the Statue of Liberty or World Trade Center hopefully would win over UJ's.

Louise, a missionary in training from England, and Heidi were going with me. Heidi was helping run the campaign; Louise and I were designated broadsiders. The Friday night before our departure, the Bible study crowd prayed for us. Flanked by prayer and blessings, we were off.

The trip started with a whimper. Louise was late; it was 6:45 a.m., and our plane took off at 8:00 a.m. The airport was at least half an hour away in good traffic. Louise was running around her apartment shoving clothes into plastic bags and trying to organize her contact cards. Heidi was furious. I watched and prayed. If we pulled this one off I really would believe in miracles.

3:30 p.m. Chicago time. We had made the flight. The first leg of our adventure was about to start: training at Moody Bible Institute. We retrieved our bags and waited for a staff member from the Chicago branch to pick us up. Like characters in *The Golden Goose*, we ran into other campaigners, who ran into more campaigners, who met up with us, until we had a small procession.

The drive from the airport was pleasant. We shared stories and swapped testimonies. Minutes ago we had been complete strangers. Now we were eternal friends. Jesus, Judaism and our desire to share the Gospel bonded us like Krazy Glue.

Although each campaigner wanted to serve God, there were other motivating forces. Some campaigners wanted to meet Messianic Mrs. Right or Born Again Prince Charming. Others were seeing if they were missionary material. I was there as a paid staff worker. My job was to encourage less experienced campaigners and reach unbelievers.

"To empty myself that is my prayer," I wrote in my journal. "To be filled with your spirit and grace. To love others passing your love along. Use me for Thy glory."

We arrived at Moody. Louise and I grabbed our bags and found the women's dorm. Our room was typical college fare: grey carpet, bare walls, one window, two beds, two desks and a closet.

That evening I spent time with a campaigner named Rissa. She was apprehensive. She had only handed out tracts a few times, and had never been to New York City. I reassured her that there was nothing to fear. God would protect us. We prayed for ourselves and the thousands of Jewish people waiting for our ministry.

Training started at 6:25 a.m. Monday morning. Despite the time difference, I awoke ready to move. I was leading calisthenics. Louise and most of the campaigners weren't enthusiastic about exercise and the early hour.

We walked over to an empty field and formed a circle. Seth, who was in charge, gave me a few words of direction before I put the group through their paces. Jumping Jacks, jogging in place and deep knee bends followed. Richard Simmons would have been proud of my effort.

After the workout, we had a few minutes to shower, change and eat. The dress code was strict: skirts or dresses for women unless we were scheduled to go on a sortie. A tract bag accompanied our outfits and became our constant companion. We were required to drag it everywhere. I suggested that my co-patriots get used to the new appendage. In two weeks they'd be in New York lugging hundreds of tracts four times a day.

Memorizing Christian Bible verses, writing postcards to supporters, and meeting the tight schedule were additional requirements. Quizzes, reading assignments, workshops and exams were dispensed daily. We were kept busy.

Our first lecture was convoluted and entitled, "The Biblical Basis of Jewish Evangelism." Seth explained that Israel had been elected by God. Her mission was to be a light to the Gentiles and to bring the message of the living God to the rest of the world. God loved the nations, and would reach them through the church if Israel failed. Israel, he told us, did fail, but God's mission remained, only now the new covenant people (believers in Jesus) were to carry out God's plan.

Seth explained that most of Israel would be restored to her divine mission; the salvation of the world hinged on it. Jewish people needed to be brought to a knowledge of the Gospel, he explained, so that they could bring the Gospel to the rest of the world.

"Jewish evangelism" was a great responsibility for the church and a mandate from Scripture, he told us. In conclusion, he said that the repentance of Israel (Israel turning from sin to God), provoked by God's grace, provided the occasion for the second coming of Christ.

I was convinced. I was psyched. I was part of God's special plan. I was ready to tell Jewish people about Jesus.

While Seth illuminated us, Heidi prepared to explain how we were going to implement our calling. Her lesson was called, "The Art of Broadsiding." Like an officer teaching cadets to use a gun, Heidi covered the basics and finer points of handing out tracts, addressed our fears, and explained how to go for the kill (get contacts). All we needed now was a street corner and a few Jewish people to target.

By the end of the training course, we understood the difference between: Orthodox, Reform and Conservative; Mishnah, Gemara, and Talmud. We learned how to define Jews, debate Jews and turn Jews into Christians.

All this talk of Jews and witnessing created a hunger for UJs. We would have plenty of opportunities to confront UJs and prove and perfect our skills. No one would go home disappointed.

Early into training our entire group traveled to Watertown Square, a central shopping area in Chicago, to watch two missionaries broadside. Apparently a policeman had hassled a few broadsiders the day before and Jews for Jesus wanted to defend (as they always do) their First Amendment Rights.

Although Christianity teaches believers to obey authority, we were taught to prayerfully resist officials if our rights were being violated. Conflicts with officers were frequent and unwelcome events. The police wanted to maintain order; we wanted to distribute tracts. Sometimes our agendas clashed. I never became comfortable with the authorities.

While other campaigners struggled on sorties and stayed up studying, I slept well and breezed through broadsiding. A semi-seasoned missionary, I was used to the work and had already covered many of the lectures. I was hungry for the Big Apple.

My struggles started two days before we left for New York City. I wrenched my ankle in a wretched gopher hole while leading jumping jacks. The move triggered an old track injury. I was incapacitated. I couldn't even work a soda machine. How was I going to pass out tracts?

Crutches became my constant companion; ice, Ace bandages and rest my medicine. Nothing, not even prayer, sped up the healing process. Returning to L.A. without first doing battle in New York was a real possibility. God didn't need me, I thought.

I got on a flight, but it was bound for N.Y.C. not LAX. I was going on Campaign. My ankle would swell and blacken and aggravate me, but I would endure. I was a team leader, and I boarded the plane with my troops. Dressed in Jews for Jesus T-shirts, we lined up and silently marched on board.

Several staff members met us in New York. Yakov was to be our leader. We gathered our bags and silently filed onto a bus. The mood shifted as we moved towards Manhattan. We were soldiers of the Lord, but we were also children of God. We broke out in song, cheering Jesus and vocalizing victory.

That year many of us stayed in the posh Dumont Plaza. The hotel was still under construction, and Jews for Jesus was able to secure rooms at an excellent rate. Although there were four of us to a room, we were happy with the accommodations.

Enjoying our hotel suite wasn't a major part of the agenda. Tract distribution started at 6:45 a.m. At 9:15 we met back at the office for breakfast and chapel. Between 11:00 and 2:00, we were distributing tracts or traveling to a sight. Lunch was served and then we had a little time off. The afternoon sortie started at around 4:00 p.m. Diner was from 6:30-7:30. Then we were sent out until about 10:00 p.m. In addition, we had to fill out contact cards, write postcards and sleep.

My first sortie was a bust. The rain forced us into a subway hole. No one was riding the trains on the weekend. The sight was dead. I called the office to switch locations. The rain had stopped, and we went to the Upper West Side.

I planted Lesley, one of my teammates, in front of Papaya King. I stationed John, my other teammate, by the subway entrance, then walked towards Lincoln Center. When I got back to the sight, John was gone. I panicked, but soon found John. He had switched corners. I scolded him for moving and encouraged him to keep broadsiding.

Sweeping (handing out tracts while you walk), I decided, wasn't a great idea. I found a corner where I could keep an eye on my teammates. Meanwhile three UJs watched me. After summing me up, they started hassling me.

"How can you believe this garbage? You call yourself a Jew? Why don't you crawl down a subway hole?" they taunted.

After finishing with me, they decided to bother John. I should have threatened to call the police, but I was too intimidated to cross my tormentors. The afternoon drained the three of us. Only a month of sorties to go, we thought.

The evening sortie was better. We went to Saint Mark's Place. Jewish people passed as frequently as taxi cabs. Neo-hippies and yuppies were out enjoying ethnic restaurants and shopping for socks, earrings, incense and books. A little over a year ago I had been one of them.

At 8:00 p.m. we broke for egg-creams and encouragement at the Astor Place Coffee Shop. John and Lesley were doing fine, but they hadn't gotten the hang of talking to contacts. I decided to demonstrate witnessing techniques on our waiter.

"What do you think about Jesus?" I asked him.

"He's coming again," the waiter replied.

"Are you going to be ready when he comes?" I questioned him.

He wasn't sure. Lesley and John prayed while I explained the Gospel. The waiter understood my words and decided to receive Jesus.

Our waiter was one of the many people that I approached during campaign. But not everyone I witnessed to was a stranger. I ran into friends from college and old colleagues from retailing. One evening I even arranged to talk to my father.

I hadn't seen my dad since March. He was in Manhattan on business. I was able to get a night off, and we made plans to meet for dinner.

After the afternoon sortie, I returned to my hotel. I scoured off street slime, deposited during three sweaty sorties, and traded my tract bag for a purse and my jeans for a dress. I wanted my father to see that I was normal, happy and well. Thinking about seeing him made me anxious. The walk to his hotel calmed me down. Today both of us admit that we had a pleasant time. I almost had my father fooled. I appeared to be doing fine.

The theme of the evening was neutrality. We discussed the family, the weather, Cape Cod and New York. We enjoyed sushi. The waiter brought the check. I glanced at my watch; I needed to go, but before I could flee my father confronted me. He wanted to know why I believed in Jesus.

I took the opportunity to share the Gospel. I tried to build a case for Jesus based on facts from the Hebrew Scriptures. He listened, but he had his own itinerary; he wanted me to question my beliefs.

"If I could prove to you that Jesus is not the Messiah would you be willing to give up believing in him?" he dared me.

"Sure," I said, completely confident in my faith and hoping that God would use my father's desire to thwart my faith as an opportunity for enlightenment. I thought that if he read the Bible he would see that Jesus was the Messiah.

"Would you be willing to put that in writing?" he asked.

"All right," I replied, hesitating just a bit.

"Here's a pen. Do you have something to write on?"

"How about this."

I pulled a blank postcard from my purse and began to

write: "If you can give me sound Biblical evidence why Jesus is not the Jewish Messiah in the Old Testament, I will give up Christianity."

The agreement left both of us hoping.

While on the East Coast, I also had a chance to see my mother. On my day off, I took a shuttle to Boston. We had only a few hours together. Like the evening with my father it almost felt like old times. We rode the swan boats and enjoyed a leisurely lunch. After lunch, just a few feet from where my mother had first heard about my exodus to L.A., we talked. Now she confronted me.

"Ellen, we need to see a family counselor," she said.

I smiled nervously, wishing I was miles instead of inches away from her and pretended I hadn't heard her. I didn't want to discuss the issue. I wanted to fly back to New York to safety.

I made it back to New York and returned to my post. Sortie followed sortie and soon campaign was over. I had learned what to do about police and how to respond when physically attacked. I had distributed thousands of tracts and gathered dozens of contacts despite my ankle. But I still couldn't face my family. My friends in L.A., proud of my feats, welcomed me back eager to hear how God had used me during campaign.

23

Jesus Was Arrested Too

On T.V., being arrested looks simple. The policeman stops the suspect, cuffs the accused, and carts the person off to jail. In reality being arrested is frightening. A policeman approaches you; you stop paralyzed by fear (although you're generating enough adrenaline to lift a small automobile). Dozens of people watch as your hands are bound and you are lead away.

Most believers never even conceive of resisting the law. (Christians are supposed to be on the side of the good guys.) The Christian Bible says, "He who resists authority has opposed the ordinance of God." (Romans 13:2) Obeying the police maintains order and a good "testimony" (Christianese for "reputation").

When I enlisted with Jews for Jesus, I didn't know I would serve God by disobeying the authorities. But ignorance of the law (of Jews for Jesus) was no excuse. I soon learned that getting busted was a real possibility. Resisting authority to preserve our First Amendment rights was a well thought out procedure.

My first major run-in with the law occurred at UCLA's Mardi Gras festival. It was a Friday night. Bible study had just ended, and I was leading a Westwood Village sortie. Yossi's message had inspired the congregation, and several members wanted to go witnessing.

I packed my car with people and tracts, and another vehicle followed me. We drove over the Hollywood Hills to Westwood and parked. The Village was hopping. Young people were circulating, shopping, eating Mrs. Field's cookies, and checking out movies and each other. Up the hill, hundreds more were gobbling cotton candy and riding the Ferris wheel.

Several of my volunteers had never been on a sortie. They were acting more like adolescent girls squealing over boys than soldiers of the Lord. I was a little nervous.

We prayed for guidance, protection and opportunities. I left half of the troops in The Village under the direction of an experienced broadsider and took the rest of the crew up to the Mardi Gras. I stationed my warriors at strategic entry points and began to circulate among the crowd.

Information about UCLA and handling officials was filed in the back of my brain like an important phone number. I wasn't prepared or expecting to implement it. My mind was fixated on the mob.

I was not alone; the police were also concentrating on the crowd. This was L.A.; gang violence could heat up like the weather. Maintaining order was a necessity not an option.

A police officer asked us to stop broadsiding. His job was to avert trouble. We were in the way and posed potential problems.

He asked nicely. I panicked, stopped broadsiding and forgot all my instructions. I didn't get his badge number, I didn't note his name, I didn't try to reason with him or ask if I was doing anything wrong. I called the office, but no one was there to help me. I was worried about my volunteers. I backed down and ended the sortie.

Once again I acted erroneously. This time there were significant repercussions. Jews for Jesus had fought for the right to hand out tracts at UCLA. My mistake jeopardized ministry territory. Jews for Jesus did not lose ground, but I lost face. Moishe wanted me to pray about being released from my commitment with the ministry.

"I'm very upset," I wrote in my journal. It continues:

> I just cried for about an hour. It's hard to admit that you've failed, messed up. God doesn't need me. Part of me feels like a big zero. I feel like I've lost everything. I came out to L.A. and dropped everything to work for Jews for Jesus. I've made some big

mistakes and it's cost a lot. I'm sorry. I just cracked under pressure and did the wrong thing.

Jews for Jesus is all I have. I can't run back to mommy and daddy. I can't trust them. Maybe you want me to go Lord. I don't know. I just want to do Your will. It hurts to get reprimanded, treated like a fool. Sometimes I feel so alone. No one seems to care. I'm so glad I have you God.

Despite my troubles, the following week of ministry work went well. I felt that God wanted me to stay with the ministry. I vowed to do a better job. The next time I encountered the police I would not back down.

I had plenty of chances to test my vows. College campuses continued to be a battle ground for First Amendment rights. The next conflict was at Pierce College. Mark, one of my co-workers, was arrested first. The next day I joined him.

We arrived on campus fully prepared to take a bust. Mark was in charge. We prayed and started broadsiding. The police arrived and started to watch us. A small crowd, finding the scene more interesting than Freshman Composition or Economics 101, gathered. A policeman approached Mark. Minutes latter we were both cuffed and sitting in the back of a black and white.

Being detained was strange and intimidating. For the first time in my adult life basic rights were denied. I was not free to go, do, or determine. The authorities dictated all.

At the station I surrendered my belongings and was publicly frisked.

Next they fingerprinted me and placed me in a holding cell along with several other woman. The cell completely fit my expectations. The dark cement room contained several thin, lumpy, bare mattresses, an open toilet and a pay phone.

Most of the other guests were being held for evading parking tickets or loitering. Several asked me what I was in for. I answered, but chose not to follow up the conversation with witnessing.

Instead, I requested some change and started making calls. I was able to connect with several people. They prayed with me, comforted me and reassured me that Yossi was on his way to bail me out. The dinner cart arrived with turkey sandwiches and shriveled peas. The meal resembled leftovers from the elementary school cafeteria and smelled as bad as my cell. I felt sick. Fortunately help arrived to spring us and buy dinner.

The showdown at Pierce continued. We kept going back and getting arrested. Being renegades bound us together, magnified our holy war and brought publicity. Satan and the police couldn't stop us. Our numbers grew, and we added witnesses, tape recorders, and cameras to document the treatment.

One pair of missionaries spent a night in jail while their wives waited, worried, and tried to explain why daddy was incarcerated. I didn't spend any more time in a cell, but I was chained to a bench for several hours next to an assortment of unsavory types.

History repeated itself. The ministry won the right to preach the Gospel at Pierce as they had on other campuses and at LAX airport. To make sure the cops would behave a law suit was waged. The insurance company, who was responsible for Pierce's judicial expenses, insured that no one touched us again. The next year at Mardi Gras, when the cops bothered me, I took a bust. I was still scared, but my fear of being reprimanded by Jews for Jesus was greater than my fear of the law.

24

Cover Girl Kidnapping

I was driving along Ventura Boulevard with some friends checking out Fifty's-style diners and Chinese restaurants. We stopped at a news stand. Frantically I searched the racks for the December 7, 1987 issue of *Newsweek*. The magazine was there, and inside was a picture of me smiling, looking as Jewish as a character in "Fiddler on the Roof."

I was a Jews for Jesus poster child. The copy above my face read, "Why can't Christmas be a Jewish Holiday?" That year, I believe, Jews for Jesus spent three million dollars to broadcast their message in publications such as *U.S.A. Today* and *The Wall Street Journal*. Thousands of people sent for more information. Many probably used the material for dart boards or kitty litter.

The ads were novel, but the idea of broadening Christ's appeal at Christmas was not. Christmas's roots have little to do with Jesus. The origins of the holiday are pagan. Romans celebrated Saturnalia and the Teutonic peoples Yule. Mingling pagan festivals and Christian holidays helped build the early church. In a similar way, Jews for Jesus incorporates aspects of traditional Judaism into Christianity in order to win converts. In addition, they take advantage of the alienation that many Jewish people feel during the Christmas season. "Christmas is for everybody," one of their ads reads. Christmas is not for everybody: Hindus, Buddhists, Jews and many others do not celebrate the holiday.

Lending my face for the campaign was easy. Yossi mentioned the idea casually as if he were asking me to light Sabbath candles or go on a sortie. I rarely declined proposals from the ministry. I certainly wasn't about to make an exception now.

Several weeks before Christmas, I drove to the

photographer with a woman who was slated to appear in another ad. Traffic was thick. We were late. I arrived flustered and embarrassed, feeling like I had let the ministry down.

My companion was photographed first. Then it was my turn. I applied lipstick, pulled on one of my favorite sweaters and shined the Star of David displayed on my chest. There would be no doubt that I was Jewish.

"O.K. Ellen, look curious," the photographer coaxed. "Great! Now smile for me. Perfect. Hold it."

The camera clicked, the lights glared, I flashed $3,000 worth of orthodontics. The photographer took rolls and rolls of film hoping for the perfect shot. I prayed one of the pictures would turn out well. I am not photogenic, but I knew God and the photographer could overcome that. We tried a few more poses, and I was done.

The picture received mixed reviews. Headquarters liked the smiling pose; Jews for Judaism did not. In response, the counter-missionary organization offered a seven week training program and increased their efforts to combat missionaries. A few friends and acquaintances mentioned that they had seen the picture. No strangers recognized me from the ad. This was L.A.; I was competing with celebrities.

My parents, probably feeling that the piece was on par with child pornography, didn't acknowledge its existence. When I told my mother about my appearance in *Newsweek* she skipped over the statement as if I hadn't mentioned it.

In contrast, my brother Howard's anger exploded across the telephone wires. "How could you do this! You know what Christmas means to us," he screamed and hung up.

For Howard, an ace toy designer, Christmas was a time of intense pain and material gain. Although sales of play fire trucks and doll kitchens could make or break him, Yuletide cheer depressed him.

As children the holiday estranged us. We wanted no part of candy canes and stockings, Christmas trees and Santa Claus, mistletoe and wreaths. We were Jews--God's separate, chosen people. We wanted nothing to do with Christmas.

Here I was advertising, advocating, advancing the holiday.

Appropriately, the *Newsweek* cover story was entitled: "Headaches New Ways to Cope." My family joined the 45 million Americans who suffer from headaches. Biofeedback, aspirin, ergot compounds and beta blockers (some of the cures suggested in the article) couldn't right their condition.

I didn't think my relationship with my family could worsen. I was wrong. The ad pushed us further apart. I received a letter from my father urging me to consider where my life was heading. I discussed it with Yossi and composed a response:

Dear Dad,

I can't say that I appreciate what you had to say although I do see that you care very much about me. First of all you have no right to impose your values on me. You offer them freely and I do not wish to embrace them. What makes you the absolute authority on values ...

I may have only lived for twenty-five years, but I am old enough to make my own choices. One thing you taught me was to be a free thinker. I have thought freely and chosen the truth. It is objective, real and concrete. Whether you believe it or not doesn't matter.

I am surprised that someone so scientific refuses to investigate the evidence for Jesus. You prefer to start with the presupposition that I am involved with a bunch of people who are manipulating and controlling me ... The only people who ever have really controlled me are actually my parents ...

Yossi encouraged me to stand up for myself and my faith to gain my family's respect. Only then would they consider Jesus, I was told.

My stance drained me. I felt completely severed from my family. The day after reading my dad's letter and speaking with my mom, I went to church and cried.

By Monday I wasn't feeling better. I received a letter from my alma mater asking for contributions in memory of a former classmate. The woman was a friend. She had been murdered in her apartment. The news shocked me. I didn't know how much more I could handle.

That night I received a phone call from Moishe. I couldn't imagine what I had done. Moishe almost never spoke to me. Now he was calling? We spoke for about two hours. Moishe told me that a member of the Board of Directors felt that the girl in the ad (me) might be kidnapped. Besides being sad I now was scared. I was afraid of my parents.

"I feel so alone sometimes, God. I wish you could wrap your arms around me in the darkness engulfing my fears," I wrote in my journal.

My co-workers and I dubbed the kidnapping scenario "Operation Kiwi" in honor of my squawking, green, finger-biting parrot. The members of Jews for Jesus became my bodyguards. Chaperons accompanied me in public. I had to have a buddy on sorties, while food shopping and even to go to the bathroom.

Members of staff knew where I was and where I was going. Yossi and I already spoke every morning. Monday to Saturday at 6:30 a.m. we read the Christian Bible, prayed and discussed my schedule. Now Yossi paid special attention to my plans. In addition, I was instructed to call the office every few hours. At least I didn't have to swallow a homing device.

Three days into Operation Kiwi, Yossi mentioned that Moishe was thinking about me going incognito, perhaps to San Francisco. "What about my caseload? What about my goals? What about the Chanukah party and New Years?" I asked myself

I called Moishe, and he told me to write my parents and tell them to leave me alone for a while. I didn't know if I could compose the letter. To add to my paranoia, Moishe outlined a list of procedures to follow in the event that someone attempted to kidnap me. If I saw a member of my family, I was to run in the opposite direction. If grabbed, I was to scream and make a scene. If abducted, I was to go on a hunger strike and repeat, "If you don't release me immediately I will never speak to my parents again."

My world bordered on the surreal. I felt part of a cosmic struggle between good and evil. At any moment Satan could squash me.

Five days into Operation Kiwi, I was driving along Oxnard Street, thinking about Christian Scriptures, when two cars collided in front of me. I felt that Satan had orchestrated the accident for me.

Two days later I was handing out tracts near a woman raising funds for the Salvation Army. She became agitated, called the police, and accused me of kicking her and taking her money. A policeman ordered me to stop broadsiding. I called Yossi, and he righted the messy situation. The next day started with a flat tire and ended with a prank phone call. I envisaged bombs from Satan exploding around me.

Chanukah was a few days later. The holiday helped me bury my troubles. Jews for Jesus' carnivals rivaled any synagogue's. We had a special service, great food and ingenious games: Cleanse the Temple, Knock the Pigs, Pin the Flame on the Menorah, Bean Antiochus (how ironic, since this Syrian king in the Chanukah story tried to convert Jews), and Draydl of Fortune. Guests could hire the Maccabean Hit Squad to knock off their friends, and children could have their faces painted. Everyone had a wonderful time. All the work I put into the event paid off. For a moment my distress disappeared.

Four days later I turned 25. Aging and remaining single scared me. "I thought about death today," I wrote in my journal. "My Dad's right: I really do hate my life. It's because I long to be with God in Heaven. First I've got to do a lot down here."

My mother had her own thoughts to share in honor of the occasion. She sent me a card which read:

Dear Ellen,

Twenty Five Birthdays. I've thought for weeks about what that means to me. And it's the memory of thousands of shared moments in 25 years.

Remembering the joy that our relationship in the past brought us, makes my heart break now. For you and I both know that the difference in what you believe and what I believe have driven us apart. Somehow I would like to create the opportunity to come together without compromising my values and ideas or yours.

Last year you made me a quilt and I felt your love in those stitches. I don't have your talent, but my stitches are these words which come from my heart.

I will always love you. Happy Birthday.

She sent me *The Art Lover's Book of Days* and a picnic cooler. The journal and cooler remained empty. The gifts reminded me of how empty, how colorless, how sad my life was. There was no place for picnics and no partner to picnic with. I had no desire to record my thoughts next to paintings, prints, photos and quotes of Matisse, Van Gogh, Chagall and Picasso. These artist had been on a quest for life--I was longing for death.

A week later my mother sent me a New Year's card. "I hope in 1988 things will change between us to help bring us together," she wrote.

I longed for my life and our relationship to improve. "I'm miserable," I wrote in my diary. "I don't have control over what's going on in my life."

New Years passed eventfully. While the rest of L.A. prepared for bed, I rose for a sortie. The Rose Bowl game and parade, which took place on New Years Day, were major outreaches for our branch. I dressed in a daze and drove to the office. A few staff members and volunteers were already there. Priming ourselves with coffee and jelly donuts, we received our instructions, loaded tract bags, filed into cars and drove to Pasadena.

Piles of parade devotees were already at the sight. Most were staked out in sleeping bags or blankets. They didn't want to hear the Gospel. We wove in and out of the crowd, stepping over bodies, trying to hand out tracts anyway. The multitude stirred with the sunrise, and a few more hands accepted our literature. After saturating the crowd we escaped before the parade cut us off.

At a volunteer's house, we consumed more coffee and watched the parade on T.V. There was a devotional and a time of prayer. After a photo session and breakfast, we were ready for battle. We regrouped, climbed back into our vehicles and drove to the Rose Bowl Game for more broadsiding.

A few nights later, I couldn't even sleep at home. I received a few more strange phone calls and a man came to my door asking for a woman named Marlene. Alarmed, I called Yossi. He didn't want me to stay at my apartment. "But Yossi I have the staff breakfast tomorrow," I protested. He insisted, and we made arrangements for Jim, one of the senior missionaries, to pick me up. Jim arrived dressed like a secret agent and whisked me away. That night I stayed with Jim and his family. I had a cold and couldn't wait to go to bed.

Someone else held the breakfast. I recovered from my cold. My parents left for a trip to India. Operation Kiwi ended. I realized how much my friends at Jews for Jesus and my family in Boston loved me.

25

I Was an Oxy-moron

"How were you, how could you, how can you be Jewish and believe in Jesus?" people asked, ask, and will ask me. "Sounds like vegetarians for meat."

Explaining and understanding how I believed in Jesus and still called myself a Jew is impossible. Today I feel Judaism and Christianity are mutually exclusive. I have chosen Judaism.

"Jews" who believe in Jesus can claim to be Jewish Christians, Messianic Jews, Completed Jews, Jewish Believers, Jews for Jesus or even Mishpachah for the Messiah. I do not feel they should label their congregations synagogues or call their spiritual leaders rabbis. To do so is deceptive. Their leaders may have an extensive Jewish background, but most of them are ordained ministers, not rabbis.

Some Jewish people are lured to Messianic services under false pretenses. A Messianic Passover is not a traditional Passover. Although kosher wine may be served at both, Jesus is mentioned only at one. If someone chooses to attend such a service it is their right. To deceive someone into attending such a service is wrong.

The first time I encountered Jews for Jesus I didn't know what I was getting into; however, I did know the service was not traditional. No one lied to me and said I was in synagogue, but my mind perceived Jewishness. The wedding of Jewish traditions and Christian theology could have taken place under a chuppah. The music, the people, the prayers all appeared Jewish. The deception was subtle. I didn't realize how profoundly different their beliefs were.

Within the last two decades, missionary groups targeting the Jews have drastically changed. Before Jews for Jesus, missionary organizations weren't reaching many Jews. Society had changed, and their methods were outdated. Pastor Martin (Moishe) Rosen, a Baptist minister, left one of these organizations (American Board of Missions for the Jews) because he felt he could be more effective.

He knew he couldn't take Jews off the street, plunk them in church, tell them to accept Christ, and announce that they were now Christians. He had to work within a Jewish framework. He printed up tracts that young Jewish people could relate to and won converts.

The first tract, written in the early 70's, was called "A Message From Squares." "Hey you with the beard! We think you are beautiful. God likes long hair and beards too ... You are brave to do your own thing," the pamphlet said, and concluded with a message about Jesus.

Millions of tracts later, Jews for Jesus is a multimillion dollar organization recognized by both Christians and Jews. Today, music, prayers, liturgy and congregations have been created to accompany and help legitimize this hybrid of Judaism and Christianity.

Many Jews for Jesus members attend Fuller Theological Seminary to obtain degrees in Jewish Evangelism. Fuller is not Brandeis. Graduates have more clout in the Christian community, not more authority to speak with Jews.

To win funds from Fundamentalists, the new "Completed Jews" act Christian enough to pass the evangelical requirements. Missionaries with Jews for Jesus appear Jewish, which many Evangelicals love because they consider Jews God's special people. (Jesus was Jewish on his mother's side.) At the same time, members of the ministry embrace mainstream Christianity. In short, I feel, we acted Christian enough to get support from the Evangelical community and felt Jewish enough to maintain our false Jewish identities.

I still looked (and look) Jewish; I still read a little Hebrew and recited the Shema, but I was a Born Again Christian. I went to church not synagogue. Church attendance was mandatory, but there was no need to force me to go. The memory of Maxine's Bible study in New York faded; I learned to love Gentile churches. If time permitted I went several times a week.

In Boston I attended a small, conservative church. In L.A. I was introduced to other flavors of Christianity. There were Lutheran Churches, Assemblies of God and Baptist congregations.

I was drawn to a large Charismatic church (a congregation that believes in divinely conferred gifts or powers such as healing people by laying hands on them and praying for them) called Church On the Way. The congregation claimed to be taking L.A. for the Lord and had already bought several blocks of real estate in the San Fernando Valley.

On UJ visits I peppered my speech with Yiddish. At church I learned to speak Christianese.

"Turn to your neighbor and say Jesus and I are glad you are here tonight," pastor Jack would instruct us. "Tell your brother or sister what the Lord has been doing in your life this week. Let's praise the Lord together and ask Jesus to open our hearts," he'd say. "Let's ask God to give us a burden for the lost."

My loneliness and pain melted as I shared my troubles with complete strangers. As brothers and sisters in Christ, we could confide in each other; we were going to spend eternity together. I'd reiterate my tales and receive a smile and a word from the Christian Bible. My faith in God was magically restored.

Once I had mastered Christianese I graduated to tongues. The term, which comes from the second chapter of Acts, refers to a strange uttering of unintelligible sounds believed to be a spiritual gift. Some Christians equate the sounds with praying in the spirit (praying just with your soul, without consciously knowing what you are saying to God).

People at Church on the Way said that God wanted to bestow the gift of tongues on me. That's all I needed to hear. I started with a few syllables and within weeks I was spitting out strings of gibberish with the rest of church.

Outside of church, I kept the tongues and Christianese to myself. Blurting out "Shun-da-la-keepo-a-ti-kliptee-goo," in the middle of a UJ visit or telling one of my contacts, in Beverly Hills, that Jesus had a plan for her life was inappropriate. We prided ourselves on being able to explain the Gospel in a way that Jewish people could understand and relate to.

Some of my co-workers had a problem with my Pentecostal penchant. They could no more understand why I'd want to raise my arms and cry "yis-te-croop-telimetio-zrani" than I could understand why they wanted to sit in a Baptist church and sing "The Old Wooden Cross."

As brothers and sisters in Christ, we accepted our differences and united with mainstream Christianity. Simultaneously, we held on to our Jewish identities like Israeli soldiers defending Jerusalem. I was a Christian who considered myself a Jew. I was an oxymoron. Today I regard "Jews" who believe in Jesus as apostate Jews because they have forsaken the Jewish faith.

The following is an excerpt from a promotional brochure, written for people in churches, explaining Jews for Jesus' position:

> Those who are involved with us know that we have not separated ourselves from the mainstream of Christianity. Each person on our staff is a member of an Evangelical congregation and, together we represent many different denominations. In theology, we are not innovative but represent mainline evangelical thought and preach the historic Gospel upon which all true Christians agree. Our front-line missionaries are Jewish and are ordained or commissioned by their own churches and approved to our ministry.

When I chose to believe in Jesus I did not fully understand what I was doing. I believed accepting Jesus made me a

"Completed Jew." But Jews believe in one God who is invisible and indivisible. Jesus was a man. Accepting him as God and accepting The Trinity disqualified me from Judaism.

Mixing Judaism and Christianity, I feel, is like mixing green and red; you get mud. Both Christianity and Judaism lose meaning. Messianic Jews change liturgy like a chef substituting cream and Parmesan cheese for tomatoes and onions in a recipe for pasta sauce. Taste and texture are transformed. Hanukkah, Passover, Yom Kippur and Purim become platforms to hawk Jesus even though the traditional meanings have nothing to do with Christ.

Much of the Jewish community is offended by the reinterpretation and misrepresentation of sacred traditions and holidays. When I was a Jew for Jesus, I read the resentment as evidence that people were hearing my message. They were not interested; they were angry.

Most of my contacts tolerated my beliefs (that's why they were willing to meet with me). I was intolerant of theirs. I pushed the Gospel like a car salesman pushing a Cadillac on a young couple who love their Jeep Cherokee. I accused UJs of closed mindedness and claimed that my position was the only way.

Beneath my Jewish face and cartoonish tracts, beneath my desire to convert Jews was the message that it's not O.K. to be Jewish. I believed that Jews who did not accept Jesus went to Hell. I now consider such thinking anti-Semitic.

26

Fund Raising Fundamentalist

"Shalom. My name is Ellen Kamentsky, and I am with the ministry of Jews for Jesus. Tonight, I'd like to share with you a presentation which is called Christ in the Passover."

I repeated these words six or seven nights a week for three weeks, reiterated them at church meetings, and practiced them in my car. The useless information is still ingrained in my brain. Three years of studying for a master's in nutrition and I retain the significance of the seder plate while I have to look up the sources of B12.

Explaining the Passover took about forty-five minutes. I introduced the mostly non-Jewish audience to maror, matzah, hatzeret and charoset. They thrilled to the sound of Hebrew prayers and laughed when I explained that the seder plate was not used for deviled eggs. I hoped that they would see the life and mission of Jesus in my explanation. But more important, I wanted them to be moved so that they would support my work. This seder was the bread and butter of my ministry.

Approximately 70% of Jews for Jesus' support comes from individuals who are often introduced to the ministry by presentations such as Christ in the Passover. Many Christians joyfully gave us money, believing that their dollars were helping to build God's kingdom.

Despite what many people think, Jews for Jesus is interested in getting their hands on Jewish souls not Jewish shekels. In fact, Jews for Jesus will not accept donations from nonbelievers. "Before giving consider receiving the gift of eternal life. Jesus wants your heart, not your money," we would tell nonbelievers.

To raise money for my income and "the work," offering talks (mini-speech preceding passing the offering plate) were built into church meetings like commercials. Three-quarters of the way through the show I scheduled a five minute break, but the audience couldn't switch the channel or get a snack. They sat, listened and followed my directions.

"Everybody have a card? Great. Now we can all join in the Jews for Jesus tradition called the tearing of the involvement card," I'd say. "Let's all fold along the perforated line. O.K., now on the count of three, let's tear our cards. Ready, one, two, three." They'd fill out the cards, and I'd explain how they could be involved.

"The first way you can help us is through prayer," I'd say, holding up the *Jews for Jesus Newsletter* so that they would know how to pray for us. "The next way is to let me help you. In the back I've brought a table full of materials that will strengthen your faith and enable you to witness to your Jewish friends," I'd say. "Finally," I'd conclude, "The last way is financially."

Whether they gave or not I encouraged people to fill out the cards. This built our mailing list. Everyone who filled out a card would receive a subscription to the newsletter and be asked to donate more money. After my plea I sat down and watched the offering plate circulate.

This entire process was called "Deputation." We were told the activity was not just a mechanism to raise funds. I memorized the following from my training manual:

> Deputation is the ministry whereby we win the hearts of God's people to our cause, encouraging them to pray, give and witness to the end that Jewish people will be saved ... When our brothers and sisters in the church join in our vision for the salvation of Jewish people, when they can be inspired and brought closer to God through our work, expect that they will then be generous with their finances.

"The secret to having enough money in your fund is NOT fund-raising--it is people-raising," Moishe wrote in a letter entitled "Keeping Your Missionary Fund Solvent."

Besides the Christ in the Passover presentation, I developed a few other talks and sang with the local chapter of the "Liberated Wailing Wall." We dressed in ugly, hot, synthetic costumes meant to imitate shtetl attire and sang "Jewish gospel" music. Our biggest hit was "Tradition." The song was a spoof of a "Fiddler on the Roof" piece that chronicled the experience of a Jewish believer after he tells his family about his faith. Amy Grant, who back than was a gospel singer, had nothing to fear--we weren't very good. People liked us anyway.

Traveling with the team was more fun than conducting meetings alone. Performing the carefully scripted Christ in the Passover was taxing. Finding the church, speaking to the pastor, and upholding the ministry added to the burden.

Heidi spent hours coaching me. Like a Hollywood director she watched me while I practiced. "Make big motions. Jewish motions. Be natural. Small motions look like nervousness," she told me. "Smile, communicate, be charming, show interest," she urged.

I memorized the fourteen-page script and learned how to stumble through the various gestures. My first performance, for two senior missionaries, received the seal of approval, and I was off to conduct my own meetings.

My first tour was in Washington State. After a year of ministry work, I welcomed the break in routine. I travelled with a woman from the San Francisco branch who had been on staff for so many years that she could practically recite the Christ in the Passover backwards. My companion had a wonderful sense of humor, and we managed to have some fun.

I flew to San Francisco, met my co-worker, and we drove to Spokane.

Except for a run-in with a snow storm, the tour passed smoothly. We covered a large percentage of the state and explored Seattle. Despite my fears, I never froze in the middle of a meeting or incurred laryngitis.

The next year, tour did not go as smoothly. This time I

was the more experienced missionary, and we were going to the cold Midwest.

I met my partner, who worked for the San Francisco branch, in Minnesota. We were two California girls shivering at the airport. We rented a car and found our way in the Twin Cities and the snow.

The next day was Sunday. While the rest of the Christian world enjoyed the Sabbath, I gave two meetings. My evening meeting was in a huge church. My message was well received. I couldn't believe that God had given me an opportunity to talk to so many people.

Several wonderful days followed, and each evening we were housed with kind believers who supported our work. We handed out tracts in the Twin Cities, and I even had a few UJ visits.

The tone of tour shifted after about a week. Maybe my partner and I were complaining too much, maybe the bitter weather was chilling my mood. I was beginning to hate church meetings. People kept asking me if I was married. I was sick of hot dishes (a common church food consisting of three ingredients, two of which are usually mushroom soup and macaroni) and bars (a common church dessert usually composed of sugar, flour, chocolate and more sugar). I longed for carrot juice and sunshine.

"Lord, am I doing the right thing with my life?" I wrote in my journal. "I feel like I need some time off. I'm going all the time. Lord what should I be doing with my life?"

The weather did more than dampen my mood. The climate made driving hazardous; we started accumulating car troubles. The first incident was minor. I dug our tires into the snow, and AAA pulled us out.

Car problems and my depression deepened. "Lord I feel like the world is caving in around me. I keep thinking that You're going to zap me," I wrote in my journal.

Three days later I almost killed myself. I was driving to pick up my partner in Owatana when I hit a whiteout. I couldn't see and lost control of the van. It sailed down the highway, skidded and landed in the midway. AAA rescued me. The car was O.K. I was fine physically, but damaged mentally. I gave a talk that evening anyway.

The next accident was far more serious. There were physical injuries and the van had to be towed away. I heard about the accident from the pulpit. In the middle of my presentation someone handed me a note with the words, "Your partner's been in a car accident."

I finished my talk and asked the congregation to pray for my friend. I packed up my materials, and a pastor drove me to the hospital.

My partner was in the emergency room waiting to be x-rayed. She looked awful, but was going to be O.K. I wasn't O.K. Two years of suppressed frustration, anger, stress, bitterness and blackness sprang from my "saved" soul. Twenty-four meetings in twenty-one days, waking at 5:00 a.m., driving miles in the snow. We had been pushed too far.

That night our housing was horrible. Neither of us got much sleep. My partner tried to recuperate. Her face was badly bruised. I think she broke a finger, and she was still in shock.

The next day I dealt with van logistics. When I returned, my partner was on the phone talking to her supervisor in San Francisco.

"Please don't make me get up and speak tonight," she pleaded over and over. "I can't do it."

I couldn't believe they were going to make her talk. For the second time in twenty-four hours I lost it. I completely sided with her. Making her speak in this condition was inhuman.

The hours passed miserably. Ice, aspirin, and rest weren't helping. My partner's face was so black and puffy that she couldn't even wear her glasses. The phone calls continued to arrive. The voices from San Francisco tried to talk her into speaking. I listened and tried to talk her out of it.

One of the voices wanted to talk to me. The voice belonged to Lisa, my old friend and my partner's supervisor.

She told me off, said I was partially responsible for my partner's attitude, and told me to shape up.

The conversation devastated me. My anger shifted from the ministry to myself. Criticizing Jews for Jesus was wrong, I thought. I was partially responsible for my partner's condition. I had sinned. I needed to repent. I begged Jesus to forgive me and change my attitude.

I don't know if Jesus ever forgave me. I tried to forgive the ministry and forget what had happened on tour, but I could not. I believed my stance was evil. Harboring poor feelings about the ministry was wrong.

I went back to L.A. determined to improve my posture. I asked God to transform me, but my problems with Jews for Jesus grew. I had begun to realize that some of my opinions about the ministry were justified.

27

Shrinking Faith

I am an adept actress. In L.A. I played the role of the happy missionary. I fooled most people including myself.

Two individuals in L.A. penetrated my facade: my podiatrist and my psycho-therapist. Both were Christians, had nothing to do with Jews for Jesus, and saw the toll the ministry was taking on me. Worried about my health, they exposed my distress. But I couldn't handle the truth, so I slipped away and back into character.

I saw Dr. Blanchard, my podiatrist, because my feet were crawling with plantar warts. The hard growths refused to disappear (even with prayer) and were spreading like mold infesting a cantaloupe. Care was imperative. Without treatment, I would have trouble walking.

I postponed the visit. I knew, from previous encounters with the virus, that treatment hurt. Every time I passed the doctor's office, which was a 1/2 a mile from my apartment, I recalled the pain. A tight schedule was my excuse. I'd sacrifice my health for "the work."

Finally ailment anxiety outweighed my fears, so I scheduled an appointment at the doctor's office. The receptionist informed me that there had been a cancelation; the doctor could see me immediately.

Dr. Blanchard walked into the waiting room, introduced himself and invited me into his office. He examined my feet and confirmed my diagnosis; I had plantar warts. He left the room and returned with an iodine-scented foot bath. I immersed my feet in the warm, auburn solution. The doctor left.

He returned and began to work on my feet and minister to my spirit. We swapped testimonies and discovered that we attended the same church. I spoke glowingly about the ministry (I had been indoctrinated to ALWAYS uphold Jews for Jesus) and my work, but the doctor sensed I wasn't being completely truthful. Dr. Blanchard had seen hundreds of cases of plantar warts; he knew that stress compromised the immune system and could aggravate the condition. My feet exposed me. The planter virus revealed that I was under tremendous pressure.

As my doctor and a fellow Christian, familiar with the work of Jews for Jesus, he urged me to reconsider my commitment. My lifestyle was harmful, he said. Car accidents, illnesses and mood swings were not normal; they resulted from stress not Satan. I was overworked. God did not want me to live this way, he said.

I listened, partially agreed with him, and even considered leaving; but my commitment to "the work" was too strong. How could I abandon my wondrous calling? How could I walk away? What other work could compare with leading people to Heaven? Wouldn't I be disobeying God? God was testing me, and the Devil was trying to break me, I thought. Adversity was the cost of serving God.

I saw the doctor a few more times. The warts withered, but the qualms Dr. Blanchard had raised remained and infected my work. A fellow Christian had affirmed my doubts. Perhaps my complaints were legitimate. Therapy would elicit the truth.

Removing the warts was a holiday compared to treating my psyche. The sessions exposed everything: eating disorders, difficult relationships, confusion, unhappiness, fear, stress, anxiety. My life embodied a thesaurus entry for the word "depression."

Moishe suggested that I see a Christian counselor to help me separate from my parents. Obviously the kidnapping scenario had failed to sever us. Neither of us thought my troubles with Jews for Jesus would be a focus of therapy.

I listened to Moishe and entered therapy to resolve parental conflicts. I was not prepared or willing to deal with the other issues. I had entered Jews for Jesus to escape problems. I didn't want to deal with them. But all the problems were woven together like clues in a murder mystery. Each needed to be exhumed and examined to solve my life.

I started seeing Christine, my therapist, twice a week. Initially I looked forward to the visits. Christine would pray and then we would spend forty-five minutes talking. I liked having someone to share my problems with. But after a few sessions, Christine pushed me to face them. Many of these problems were associated with the ministry.

Eating disorders were a symptom, not a cause of my problems. The behavior, characterized by complete lose of control, scared me.

I struggled to regulate every minute of my life. On a typical day I woke at 5:30 a.m., went jogging, spoke to Yossi at 6:30, prayed with staff at 7:30, wrote postcards at 8:00, rushed to visits at 9:00, was on a sortie by noon, and that was just the morning.

Some evenings the tension, generated by trying to hold my life together, overwhelmed me; and I'd raid the refrigerator for relief. Food was a safety valve, a substitute for love, a way to anesthetize myself and stuff my feelings.

After a binge I'd feel guilty, sinful, sick. The next day I vowed to fast or guard my eating habits. I'd pray for God's help, but the pattern repeated. My body, once my friend, was the enemy, ready to trip me and separate me from God the way it had done for Eve after she ate the apple in the Garden of Eden.

I had lost control of my life. Before I joined Jews for Jesus, I was beginning to take charge of my destiny. I was exploring careers and my identity. Troubles in New York overwhelmed me, and I allowed the ministry to take control of my life. In the process I lost the troubles temporarily, but I also lost the ability to determine my future.

Eventually the troubles resurfaced. Jesus might have made me a new person, but the new creation in Christ had the same problems as the old Ellen.

Christine pointed out that the ministry was controlling me.

When I wasn't the person they wanted me to be, I was punished. I had cut off my thoughts, feelings and emotions. I didn't explore options. I didn't have the space to think and people to discuss alternatives with. I didn't have the leisure to contemplate my life. I just kept running to sorties, to visits, to meetings, to the phones, to avoid thinking.

Problems with the ministry crept into therapy. Unlike my visits with the foot doctor, no medicine was available to shrink the problem. The solution involved breaking away from Jews for Jesus. I wasn't prepared to do that, so I terminated therapy.

Meanwhile my parents were taking significant steps to improve our relationship despite the ministry's attempts to sabotage it. My mother and father had intervened too often and influenced me too much in the past. Was a mature relationship possible? Ironically, my parents acknowledged the need to let me go, while discussing how to intervene and free me from Jews for Jesus. A mature relationship could only follow emancipation.

On Mother's Day 1988, I received an article from my mother entitled, "Post-Child Mothering." The essay, by Ellen Goodman, expressed my mother's difficulties in parenting me. Knowing when to nurture, when to interfere, and when to set me free was hard. She missed, as the article put it, "the pleasure of each other's company."

I missed the walks, the trips to New York, the hours deciphering contemporary art and fixing newfangled food. I feared one day we would be strangers. We had been entering a very special friendship denied my mother and my grandmother. Would my mother and I repeat the pattern?

My mother sent me a letter, near the anniversary of her mother's death, expressing her feelings over the loss of both her mother and her daughter (me):

Dear Ellen,

I was touched by your concern about my

```
sadness. Yes, I'm always sad about the loss
of my dear Mother, because we never had a
chance to develop a relationship as adult
to adult which I know would have been
extraordinary. She died when I was 25, and
the whole year preceding her death, she no
longer even recognized me. But my sadness
is so much greater now, because in this
last year I began to feel that you and I
were beginning a new relationship as two
adults who care so much about each other.
If you were me and wanted desperately to
mend the link between us, what would you
do?
```

I didn't know what to do. I knew that I hurt. I missed my mother. I missed my friend.

My father's absence was equally agonizing. His distress was more suppressed. For years we had shared thoughts and a mutual love for science, nature, philosophy and each other. Now we shared speech without meaning. Science, philosophy, politics, knowledge meant nothing to me. We had lost common ground. We had lost our relationship.

For the first time in my life, my father wrote long letters to me composed on the PC. The gesture touched me as much as his words. The letters were filled with details about the finches that lived in my mother's geranium, the weather on Cape Cod and his new office in Cambridge.

Between the lines, he planted thoughts which bore into my memory and dredged up old values. "Kate [my brother's girlfriend] was impressed with the seder and the emphasis on universal liberty and freedom," he wrote. "Lee returned from the CIA protest march in Washington against our Central American involvement," he wrote in another letter. "Do you have time to read as widely as you used to?" he asked in yet another.

He fished for ways to show he cared: How is your new

car? Your apartment? Your cat? The letters always ended the same way: "We all miss you, stay in touch, take care of yourself, love, Dad."

I could run away from my problems, but not from my parents. They never lost touch. They never lost hope. My father wrote:

I want nothing more, and I have always looked forward to getting to know you, relate to you as an adult, and to enjoy together all of the blessings of life that will come to our family. We are at a terrible impasse that does not allow this to be possible because we are confused about who you are, what you really believe, and how you want to relate to your family. I believe with mom that the only hope to save our family is family counseling, and I am certainly willing to be a part of it. I believe in you and know you too want to bring our family back together.

He was right. I wanted to bring the family back together.

28

Witness at the Wedding

Wonderful events occurred while I was in L.A. My brother Lee became a father and my brother Howard got married.

I first heard about Cheri, Howard's wife, through the mail. "I'm doing my laundry tonight," Howard wrote me. "I'm trying to be better about keeping in touch with friends, so every week I'm writing a letter. This week it is to you."

The colorful letter was filled with news about Howard's new studio, haircut, band and girlfriend. "This is definitely the big 'L'," he informed me. "She's eclectic, lives on the 5th floor of my building with her two black cats, and does large abstract paintings," he wrote. To round-out the image he included a pen sketch of Cheri with the caption: " < --- looks exactly like this."

Howard's feelings for Cheri were more accurate than his sketch. Cheri hardly resembled Howard's drawing, but the cartoon portrayed his fondness for her. The photos, which arrived a few weeks later, were far more flattering.

Pictures of the whole family arrived at my mailbox as reliably as sweepstake offers. There were snapshots of my mom and dad, Howard and Cheri, and Lee and Kate, on Rosh Hashanah, The Fourth of July and Thanksgiving, taken on the Cape, in restaurants, and in Boston. The idea was to made me homesick; the plan was working.

My family grew and enjoyed life despite my absence. I watched them develop through pictures like a soap opera fan following "Days of Our Lives." My spirit mingled with the images like an apparition. Three years of birthdays and dinners, picnics and parties. These missed events are not redeemable.

Howard and Cheri's relationship deepened. Lee and Kate

prepared to have a child. Howard and Cheri were engaged. Kate became pregnant. My brothers relayed the news. I was happy for them and sad that I couldn't be in Boston to share their joy. The wedding date was set for August of 1988. The baby was due in April of 1989.

I wasn't present at the birth, and I almost didn't make the wedding. About a week before the ceremony, I received a call from Moishe. He was concerned that my family might try to pull something during the festivities.

Moishe's apprehension alarmed me, but the idea of their kidnapping me during the wedding was ridiculous. I knew my family better than Moishe. My parents would never force me to speak with someone about my involvement with the ministry. They were not going to employ the wedding to divorce me from Jews for Jesus. I posed more of a threat to them than they did to me. They were afraid that I would bring Jesus as my date and insist on introducing him to the wedding party.

But Moishe's feelings were not unjustified. He had seen families struggle to extricate relatives. He knew my family wanted me back. And he was right. Four months before the wedding, my mother persuaded me to talk to a "family counselor" who the ministry suspected was an anti-missionary. To my family's disappointment, the incident ended uneventfully. I told the man my story, he listened and tried to act as a mediator. Meanwhile the ministry half expected never to see me again.

Moishe's words were clear. He wanted me to establish exactly where I would be staying during the wedding. I called my brother and mother, but they had no idea where we were being housed. Cheri's family had not made the arrangements yet. Moishe advised me to declare an ultimatum: If my family didn't reveal the whereabouts of our hotel, I wasn't going.

I recalled the Hell I had undergone the last time I had listened to Moishe. For six weeks, following my appearance in *Newsweek*, I was tethered to Jews for Jesus and terrified of my parents. I wondered if the entire kidnapping scenario had been fabricated. Was this another touch to damage my relations?

For the first time I said "no" to Moishe.

"I can't believe you could be so stupid," he said, and hung up the phone.

I was upset. But I had missed my best friend's wedding because of the ministry, and I wasn't going to miss Howard's.

My appraisal of the circumstances was correct. No one attempted to kidnap me or dampen my faith, and I took full advantage of the situation by witnessing to as many people as possible. The opportunity was outstanding; most of the guests were Jewish.

Like a secret agent, able to pass for a native on foreign soil, I infiltrated the crowd and planted Jesus bombs. In another situation my strikes would have been frustrated. My cover was perfect. The rest of the wedding party was happy to talk to the groom's sister. I felt unstoppable.

"So far everything at the wedding is going well. God is blessing us so much. I pray, Lord, that they will ALL come to know You," I wrote later in my journal. "No confrontations PTL (praise the Lord). I've also witnessed to some of Cheri's family PTL. Some of them were interested. God, please use me as You see fit."

In reality the guests were just tolerating me. No one was interested in hearing about Jesus.

Cheri's family kept us busy all weekend. We ate well and were treated to a tour of Detroit. We joked over beers, feasted on thick deli sandwiches and visited historical sights and art museums.

The simple service took place in a small sanctuary. The two sets of parents gathered with the young couple under the chupah to reenact the traditional ceremony. At the mention of God, I was reminded that no one knew Jesus. I prayed silently for Cheri and Howard's happiness and salvation. The few times that I attended Jewish services, I always felt sad because God was mentioned without Jesus.

With the smash of a glass and a chorus of mazel tov the service was over. We formed groups and drove to a local restaurant to celebrate. A party in honor of the couple was held the next day. In my conservative dress I felt ugly, and I envied the woman wearing frilly, sexy outfits. I tried to ignore the alcohol, but it's presence reminded me that I was misplaced.

Despite my belief in Jesus, Cheri's family treated me like mishpachah. I was surprised that people who didn't know Jesus could be so loving. The entire weekend was delightful; leaving was distressful. I didn't want to go back to L.A. I didn't know when I would see my family again or if I could continue to do "the work."

I tried not to cry, but I felt so alone. I turned my back on old and new family and walked towards the terminal.

29

One-way

"Why do you want to go home? Your family will make you miserable? Why waste the one week of vacation you have?" my co-workers asked me.

The answer arrived on April 27th, 1989. He weighed 7 pounds, eight ounces. His name was Daniel Sean Kamentsky, my nephew. I wanted to meet him. I wanted to hold him. I wanted to be part of his life; I wanted him to be part of mine. I went home to see Daniel and the rest of my family. As soon as I got there I didn't want to leave.

The Friday night before my trip home, I cut services short and drove to LAX airport with a friend. With the Christian Bible in hand, I boarded my red-eye flight to Boston. Nervous and anxious, I found my seat and tried to relax.

There was a stopover in Newark. I had slept for only about three hours, but I prided myself on needing little rest. I usually slept six hours a night. That's all I thought I needed.

The crowd and glaring lights intensified disorientation and fatigue. I found the mobbed ladies' room and carved out a space before one of the mirrors. I pulled out toothbrush, comb, and mascara and coaxed in my contact lenses. I desperately wanted to look right. Maybe then my parents would stop trying to convince me that I was destroying my life.

The flight to Boston left in an hour. I found a coffee shop filled with the aromas of New York--fresh muffins, brewed coffee and huge bagels. The fragrance was familiar, comforting. I'd spent much of my life in New York. But Jesus had taken me away from my old existence, and so with Valley Girl style I ordered 1/2 a cantaloupe and a cup of herbal tea.

It was time for my flight. Next I was airborne and cruising

over Long Island Sound. The flight attendants barely had enough time to serve orange juice before the captain announced that we were landing. I had ten minutes to assemble my thoughts and prepare to meet my mother and father.

The plane coasted to a stop at 6:50 a.m. My parents were at the gate, looking great the way loved ones do when you haven't seen them for a long time. We walked to the car hugging the entire way as if the wall of dogma surrounding me didn't exist.

The car was packed with coolers, beach toys, and reading material for Cape Cod where we intended to spend the week. I couldn't wait to get there. My mother and I had picked out each swatch of fabric at our beach house. I had built the clay pots and soap dishes, shaped like fish, scattered through the rooms. Over a banister hung the quilt I had given my mother a few days before slipping away to L.A.

Entering the house produced a mixture of happiness and dread. For a week I could relax, but in an instant the vacation would be over and the ordeal in L.A. would resume. In addition I had to pretend that my life as a follower of Jesus was wonderful so my family would want to become Christians too.

The only person who did not see past the facade was Daniel, my family's lethal weapon aimed at pulling me away from Jews for Jesus.

Dan and I met for the first time shortly after my arrival. Toothless, he smiled at me from the protective walls of his baby carrier. He was oblivious to my existence. I was instantly smitten. How could I go back to L.A. and see my baby nephew grow up in pictures?

Howard arrived a few hours later. The whole family was now together. That afternoon we ate and swam and tanned and ate again, joking and talking as if we had never been separated by 3,000 miles and fundamentally different beliefs.

Saturday night my mother created an incredible bouillabaisse overflowing with lobster, monk fish, muscles and clams. We opened wine and stayed up playing dominos and cards. The bonds between us were being repaired despite our separate agendas. I wanted them to see that I was normal and grow curious about my faith; they wanted to liberate me so I could lead a normal life.

Monday morning the house was quiet and empty. My brothers were back in Boston. My parents and I were left to enjoy the week together. I woke and went to the window to look out. The sky was cloudless. It was the kind of day that New Englanders pray for and Southern Californians take for granted.

My parents were in the kitchen eating Wheaties and preparing toast and coffee. I joined them, and we discussed how to spend the day.

After breakfast, we drove North along Route 6 to the National Sea Shore. We parked and walked along a narrow path obscured by beach grass. The trail took us to a simple structure grayed from years of salt and wind. We captured the shadows with our cameras and created stories to explain the abandoned building's existence.

Lunch time arrived. We drove to Provincetown and ate at a casual joint along the beach. My father and I split a pizza, one of the few things we had shared in years.

Provincetown was crowded with tourists, buying string bikinis to frame their tans, and children devouring fudge and penny candy. We stopped at the army surplus store to see if they still sold marbles by the handful and moldy sea rations from WWII.

The afternoon ended with the sun melting into Cape Cod Bay, turning the world orange, gold, and indigo. The dreamy day was over.

Tuesday I woke to the sound of rain. The harmless moisture, I feared, would trap us in the house for days. The congeniality simply couldn't continue.

At breakfast my fears materialized. My father told me how my involvement with Jews for Jesus had affected him.

"Ellen, our life hasn't been the same since you joined

Jews for Jesus. I think about you every day. Mom and I are very concerned about your well-being. You just aren't the same person anymore. Everyone misses you and wishes that we could come together as a family. I'm worried that you are jeopardizing your future and your relationship with me and everyone else in the family," he said.

"Ellen, I agree with your father," my mother said. "I'm very upset about what has come between us. I feel like we really need to talk over our problems and differences."

"I thought we were getting along fine," I said.

"The last several days have been nice," she said. "This is the first time in three years that we've been able to just enjoy spending time together, but there still is a lot of work that needs to be done before we can come together as a family."

"I think things can continue to get better between us," I said.

"We still aren't as open and honest as we used to be with each other. You've told us a little about the troubles that you're having in California and how much you miss being part of the family. Mom and I really want to help you resolve some of these issues," my father said. "We want you to understand that we are thinking differently too. Your faith in Jesus is not the issue. The undue influence that Jews for Jesus is having on you is what concerns us."

"I know I have problems with Jews for Jesus," I admitted. "But I don't think that you and mom can help me. When I get back to L.A., I'll talk with someone."

"Do you really think that will help?" my father asked. "Don't you see how they are controlling you. You'll get back to California and nothing will change."

"I don't know. What am I supposed to do? I can't leave."

"Maybe we can talk about your problems the way we used to before you joined Jews for Jesus. You've become terribly narrow-minded. This weekend was the first time that you actually were talking to us like a normal person. We're your family. You can trust us. They've got you convinced that we're monsters. You'll get back to L.A., and they'll keep running your life."

"Lou, calm down," my mother interrupted.

"Sorry, I can't help it," My father said. "Thinking about how they are controlling her makes my blood boil."

I didn't know what to do, but I decided to confide in my parents. "It's not easy living out there by myself," I said. Sometimes I really want to quit. I miss everyone. I miss just relaxing and enjoying myself. They keep me so busy. Sometimes I really hate it. I wish I had more control over my life."

I felt doomed. In a few days I would be back in L.A. My week at the Cape would be a memory. Daniel would grow up and take his first steps without me. The next time I saw him and the rest of the family we would hardly know each other. I would watch the family celebrate and change through pictures. My face would remain absent.

In L.A. the pressure would start again. Goals and responsibilities would increase. Loneliness would continue. But God wanted me in Jews for Jesus. How could I leave?

"You can get help," my mother said. "You have choices. Don't you think you should think over what you are doing? Consider where your life is going, Ellen."

"Mom, you just don't understand. It's not that easy."

"Your father and I and Lee and Howard love you very much. We're all here to support you. When I told Lee and Howard you were coming up for the weekend, they dropped everything to be here. You know that we all care about you."

"I appreciate what you're saying. But no one in the family understands my situation. None of you can help me. What am I supposed to do--quit? I have responsibilities. I have a life in L.A. I have to go back."

"Would you consider talking to someone outside the family?" my mother asked. "Maybe a counsellor could help you and help bring us together."

"I don't know."

"I think we all need to sit down with someone else and discuss what has happened between us."

"All right, if you really think it will help, I guess I would be willing to talk with someone."

Before the words were out of my mouth, my mother was out the door. She had hired an exit-counsellor who was waiting in a motel room across town and went to pick him up.

My father, being careful to avoid discussing my mother's disappearance, continued to talk with me. He focused on the battery of problems that I was having in Jews for Jesus and encouraged me to open up.

Meanwhile the missionary Ellen was getting upset.

"What about your commitment to the group?" the missionary Ellen asked me. "What about all you are doing for the Lord? "Ellen, you can't leave Jews for Jesus--you will be disobeying God."

But the exorcism had started.

Twenty minutes after my mother's exit, the ghost buster arrived. He was an Orthodox Evangelical Christian and an expert on cults and destructive religious groups. He had two huge metal suit cases filled with video tapes on aberrant organizations and an even larger heart.

"This is David Clark," my mother said, offering no further explanation.

With the introduction complete, David sat down with me and started a monologue, which continued for the next two hours, and a dialogue, which continued for four days.

He told me about the years he had spent in a destructive Christian group. The organization had ruined his life and driven a friend to suicide.

"One day Winnie just couldn't take the pressure, which the group was putting on her, anymore. She locked herself in her bedroom and took her own life," he said. "That's when I left. It took me a while to understand what had happened, but after a few years I understood how the group had abused me."

I listened politely; my parents watched. David's story was horrible, but what did it have to do with me and my problems? I was tired of listening to him. What he was saying wasn't helping me. I resented spending my vacation with this stranger. I wanted to enjoy my time off; the missionary Ellen, feeling threatened, wanted David to leave.

"Ellen, your parents and I suspect that Jews for Jesus has too much control over your life," David said. "They've asked me to talk with you and discuss what you are doing in L.A. Frankly, I don't know very much about Jews for Jesus. I'm hoping you can tell me more about your experience."

Immediately I felt sick. I couldn't hide the truth about my involvement with Jews for Jesus from myself, my parents or David anymore. I knew that they were right. Jews for Jesus was controlling my life. But the pain of acknowledging the truth was incredible, and the prospect of questioning my life in L.A. and taking action to change my situation was equally distressing.

I decided not to run. I decided to confront my problems and question Jews for Jesus. The missionary Ellen started to panic. She knew that the real Ellen was about to dissect her. My friend's car accident during tour in Minnesota had primed me. I was ready for the operation.

I began to open up and talk about my troubles. Instead of admonishing me for my poor attitude the way Jews for Jesus had, David listened and sided with me instead of the ministry. Why was a fellow Christian not supporting my involvement with Jews for Jesus? Didn't Christians think members of Jews for Jesus were God's gift to the world?

David was gentle, but firmly pointed out the controls that the group had on me. "Don't you see how they have been overworking you?" he asked. God doesn't want you to be killing yourself spreading the Gospel. Whether or not someone comes to believe in Jesus is up to Him. He uses us, but he wants us to take care of ourselves too."

"It's really tough for me to take care of myself. I work so hard. I feel like nothing is ever good enough. When I try to relax, I think about all the people I need to talk to; or I worry about my goals."

"Don't you see, they keep you so busy that you can't

think. You're under too much pressure. That's not how Jesus wants us to live. Where are the fruits of the Spirit? Jesus promised us peace and joy and love. That's not what you're getting."

"I really can't take much more of it. Sometimes I'm so stressed out that I can't even function. We're all so tired that we are always getting in car accidents. A few months ago I crashed my car into another vehicle. I was just going to the health club. I wasn't even going very fast. Stacy totaled her car, and Jeff's been in a bunch of accidents. Fran (another missionary) and Jeff both have terrible back problems because of their accidents. I'm scared that something might happen to me. Sometimes I want to get in an awful accident so I won't have to go on."

"Ellen, this really doesn't sound right to me."

"I know that it's not right, but what am I supposed to do? I can't leave the ministry. God wants me to stay in Jews for Jesus. I'm afraid of violating God's will for my life."

"Ellen, don't you see Jews for Jesus has you thinking that your relationship with God is tied to them. Leaving Jews for Jesus doesn't mean that you are leaving God."

At the word "leaving," the missionary Ellen started to get upset.

"I can't leave. What else can I do with my life?" the missionary Ellen pleaded. "I don't want to jeopardize my relationship with God."

"There is a lot more to your relationship with God. You've been given mainstream Christianity with Jews for Jesus specifics. Do you really understand the difference between what is Jewish and what is Christian? You haven't been able to question anything because you are always surrounded by members of the group."

David was right, but I couldn't listen anymore.

"I really need to take a break from this."

"Sure, I think that's a great idea."

I was a little surprised at David's response to my request. He wasn't telling me what to do. He was being reasonable.

David's treatment was a revelation in itself. I wasn't used to people giving me space. I grabbed my sneakers and went for a run.

When I returned it was time for dinner. We drove to a nearby lobster restaurant. The four of us thoroughly enjoyed the meal. The conversation lightened up, and I realized in Jews for Jesus I had never been able to enjoy simple pleasures because I was always under so much pressure.

David and I kept working after dinner. I continued to swing from one extreme position to another. One minute I was excited about leaving the group, the next I was worried that if I left my life would be a total loss. I was fearful about what lay ahead.

"Lord, I just want to follow You!" I wrote in my journal. "My whole world's been turned around. I spent the entire day in dialogue with David Clark who feels Jews for Jesus is abusing me. I agree with what he says. I've decided to leave the ministry. Lord, is it right? Please direct me."

The next morning, I woke up early and called Lee and Howard to tell them about my decision to leave Jews for Jesus. They both were thrilled and relieved. I was happy that they were back in my life and knew that I could rely on them in the future.

My declaration of independence was liberating.

"I'm free. I'm out," I yelled to my parents and David. My father started to cry. It was the best news he had ever heard. My mother started to cheer and dance around the house. David joined the celebration.

My attitude was completely different. I began to critically analyze the ministry. David helped. He got out his suit cases and started showing me tapes. We spent the morning watching and discussing a debate on "Sally Jessy Raphael" between Rabbi James Rudin and two members of Jews for Jesus. I felt the members of Jews for Jesus came across as foolish, narrow-minded and obnoxious. The viewing enabled me to analyze and explain what people in Jews for Jesus were trained to do.

I knew that I had to leave, but I was still scared to do it.

"I'm really glad that I'm finally leaving," I told David. "I'll just go back to L.A., give my notice and finish up my commitment."

"I don't think that's such a good idea," David said.

"Why not?"

"Once you get back to L.A., Jews for Jesus is going to employ all kinds of tactics to try and get you to stay."

"But I'll tell them I quit."

"Ellen, you don't fully understand the kind of control that they have over you."

"But I have to go back. I have meetings to give. I have my caseload. I need to tie up lose ends."

"Going back to L.A. would be very dangerous. If you go back there, it will be very hard to leave. They will try to convince you that everything we've talked about is a lie."

"But what about all of my stuff. I have to go back. I have to say goodbye to people."

"Maybe one of your brothers can get your stuff for you."

"I don't know why this is so important. I really feel strong enough to leave on my own."

After arguing a little more and thinking about David's points, I decided to take David's advice. I prepared to call Yossi and tell him I wasn't coming back. I dialed L.A. Yossi answered the phone.

"Hi, Yossi," I said.

"How are you kiddo?" he asked. "Are you enjoying your vacation?"

"Well, Yossi not exactly."

"Is something wrong?"

"Well, Yossi, I'm leaving the ministry."

"Wait a minute. What do you mean?"

"Yossi, I'm leaving. I quit."

Yossi was shocked, upset and speechless. He had never seemed shaky like this before. Yossi always had a response. Yossi always knew what to say. Clearly this was a new problem which he wasn't sure how to address. Yossi wasn't used to the real Ellen who could make important decisions without his input.

Several hours later, the phone rang. My mother answered. It was Yossi. He wanted to talk to me. My mother asked me if I wanted to speak with him. I decided to take the call.

The Yossi I spoke to was different than the man I had talked to earlier. He was calm and had an agenda. I suspect he had spoken to Moishe and was delivering the director's ultimatum. He told me that if I wasn't on the plane on Saturday I should consider myself dismissed. I felt like asking, "If Moishe wants to talk to me why doesn't he call me directly instead of having you speak for him?"

The spell was broken. I found the incident ludicrous. I had quit, and Jews for Jesus was giving me a chance to change my mind? Hadn't Yossi heard me? I didn't want another chance. They couldn't have the satisfaction of dismissing me. The decision to leave was mine.

David and I talked about my conversation with Yossi. The interaction with my ex-supervisor confirmed that my decision to leave Jews for Jesus was right.

My parents, David and I spent the afternoon watching more videos. We looked at films on televangelists, Christian cults, such as the Bible Speaks, and a piece on the Moonies. David helped me analyze and criticize these groups. I couldn't believe how these groups paralleled my own experience. David also explained how "Hebrew Christians" distorted both faiths, and I agreed with a lot of what he was saying.

Thursday I woke up much more relaxed. I was beginning to feel more comfortable with my decision and my mood swings were less severe. I couldn't believe that I didn't have to go back to L.A. I still wasn't sure how to completely extricate myself.

I decided I needed to call my friend Stacy. I asked her about my cat. She said that she didn't feel right about going into my apartment any more and had given the keys to my landlord. She wouldn't even feed my cat. She had very little to say to me. She was acting like a robot.

"Ellen, why are you doing this. This doesn't sound like you," she said.

Stacy was partially right. I did not sound like the woman she had known in L.A. That person no longer existed. I had uncovered Jews for Jesus and discovered myself.

Epilogue

Learning to ask and answer my own questions has been a significant part of my recovery. When I left Jews for Jesus, simply handling daily decisions such as when to wake up and where to go was difficult: I had been told what to do for so long.

David enabled me to walk away from Jews for Jesus; now I had to rejoin mainstream society. Unbound, an organization which helps victims of cults and destructive religious groups, entered to help me with re-entry.

I arranged to have my belongings transported from L.A. and booked a flight to the Midwest where Unbound was located. Kevin Crowly, the head counsellor at Unbound, met me at the Iowa City airport.

We arrived at the comfortably furnished house where I was to spend the next two weeks recovering from my ordeal. Kevin introduced me to other staff members and handed me an outline of the "House Rules" (compare these with Heidi's rules in chapter 14):

1. YOU HAVE THE RIGHT TO LEAVE.

2. You have the right to disagree with anyone.

3. You have the right to relax.

4. You have the right to question any of us about our own beliefs and how we came to hold them.

5. You have the right and the responsibility to use your time here to your own best advantage, whatever that may be.

The rules felt strange. No one woke me at 6:30 a.m. to read the Christian Bible. There were no goals to meet; no one told me what to do. The freedom was unfamiliar. I expected

Kevin and the other staff members to regulate my schedule, but no one scheduled anything unless I first asked for it.

I studied mind control and began to understand my experience with Jews for Jesus. I watched films about cults and read books on comparative religions, relationships and rites of passage. We went bowling, played pool and hung out at greasy spoons. I had fun and began to feel normal.

"For the first time in a long time I finally feel like me," I wrote in my journal. "I'm also happy. Not the giddy unstable feelings I had in the group, just content and good. I don't feel like I have all this weight pressing down on me."

Unbound smoothed my transition from ministry to mainstream society, but it would take much more to recover.

"I'm scared. I've been back in Boston for a few hours, and I feel like where I was many years ago: living with my parents, unemployed, unsure," I wrote in my journal after returning from Iowa. "I have plans, but part of me wants to curl up into a ball and die. I feel burnt, embarrassed and confused. I'm not sure what to do with myself."

I found a good therapist and began to face my problems. I started working as a nutrition assistant and enrolled in night classes. I joined a food co-op, went to dances and made friends. I started answering the question: What are you doing for yourself?

A few people from Jews for Jesus tried to contact me. I did not respond and gradually the ministry faded from my life as I faded from theirs.

I wondered how they rationalized my departure. Two months after leaving Jews for Jesus, I received a letter from Moishe Rosen which helped answer my question:

Dear Ellen,

As you know, I haven't communicated to you since you left the ministry. I'm not writing to tell you of my personal disappointment or how all of us were quite discouraged at the way that things happened. But I will say this, that your defection made our position a lonelier one. The unfortunate thing is that it introduced an element into the staff that we never had before. That is, that before we had always counted on our colleagues being strong and as committed to the work as we are.

I have no idea of the process that you've been put through, except to believe that you've been processed. This was seen in your anger at Yossi or insistence that you'd been brainwashed, and your discovery that your parents had loved you all along and were accepting of your faith, only disapproving of "proselytizing." We've only had three or four conversations, but the woman who defected was not the same woman that I had talked to earlier.

Yes, we're hurting, because people are asking one another, "Would I ever turn my back on my calling?" ... You've made your choices, and this might surprise you, but I think they were right choices--right for God and right for Jews for Jesus. Because, if you could change your mind so quickly and easily, after having been with us and knowing what we teach, and knowing what our policies are, then you really don't belong ...

Moishe is right; I don't belong, but not because something is wrong with me, but because many things are wrong with Jews for Jesus. Within the group there is no legitimate way to leave, so I must be explained away, discredited, forgotten, or kept alive as an example to scare potential defectors. Like a rape victim who becomes the accused, I must be tried and found guilty to clear Jews for Jesus' name.

In my heart, there is a wondering about where it will all end. The words are Moishe's written to me. I don't know where this will end, but I continue to live my life in shades of grey.

Appendix A

Glossary of Jewish Terms

This glossary is provided to help readers unfamiliar with Jewish terms used in this book.

Afikomen: A piece of matzah which is hidden by an adult during the Passover seder for children to find.
Bar Mitzvah: A ceremony for Jewish boys at age 13, symbolizing passage into adulthood. (The ceremony can take place later in life.)
Bat Mitzvah: A ceremony for Jewish girls equivalent to the Bar Mitzvah.
Challah: Traditional braided bread eaten on the Sabbath.
Chanukah: Eight-day Jewish holiday which celebrates the triumph of the Jews over Syrian domination.
Charoset: Mixture of nuts, apples, cinnamon and wine eaten at the Passover seder. Symbol of the mortar used by slaves to do Pharaoh's construction.
Chavurah: An informal Jewish study/worship group.
Chometz: Food products (bread, cookies, etc.) containing leaven, not eaten during the week of Passover.
Chuppah: The wedding canopy under which Jews are married.
Conservative: The denomination of Judaism which is more liberal than Orthodox Judaism and more traditional than Reform Judaism.
Draydl: A four sided top used to play a game of chance during Chanukah.
Elijah: A prophet, believed to precede the coming of the Messiah. Referred to in the Passover seder.
Gemara: Part of the Talmud. The commentaries on the Mishnah.
Hamashiach: The anointed one: the Messiah.

Hatzeret: Whole bitter herbs, usually horseradish, for the Passover seder. See Maror.
High Holidays: Yom Kippur and Rosh Hashanah.
Hillel: Jewish centers on college campuses.
Kipah, Kipot (pl): A skullcap worn by Jewish men (now sometimes women) to show respect to God.
Klezmer: Music of Eastern Europe influenced by American jazz, played on instruments such as the clarinet and violin.
Kosher: Permitted foods to be eaten according to Jewish law.
Latkes: Potato pancakes, fried in oil, eaten during Chanukah.
Lantzman: Kinsman: fellow countryman.
Manischewitz: Manufacturer of kosher products e.g. matzah, wine.
Maror: Bitter herbs used at Passover seder. Symbolizes the bitter lives of Jews as slaves in Egypt.
Matzah: Unleavened bread usually eaten during Passover.
Matzah Ball: A dumpling made from matzah meal, usually served in chicken soup.
Mazel tov: Congratulations.
Menorah: An eight-armed candelabrum lit on Chanukah.
Mashiach: The anointed one: The Messiah.
Meshugge: Crazy.
Mezuzah: Literally doorpost. A capsule containing the Shema and parts of Deuteronomy. It is placed on Jewish doorposts to honor the Biblical commandment, "You shall love the Lord your God with all your mind, with all your strength, with all your being. Set these words, which I command you this day, upon your heart ... inscribe them on the doorposts of your house."
Mishnah: The core part of Talmud. Rules of life extrapolated from Torah.
Mishpachah: Family.
Oneg Shabbat: Literally: Sabbath delight. A gathering with food that takes place after Sabbath services.
Orthodox: The strictest and most traditional branch of Judaism.
Passover: Pesach festival which commemorates the Jewish

deliverance from slavery in Egypt during the time of Moses.

Passover Seder: The festive meal and service held on the evenings before the first and second nights of Passover.

Purim: A happy celebration commemorating the triumph over the Persian empire's plan to destroy the Jews. The story appears in the Book of Esther in the Bible.

Reform: The most liberal, modern (early 19th century) interpretation of Judaism.

Rosh Hashanah: Jewish New Year.

Seder Plate: A plate with compartments for the symbolic foods used during the Passover service.

Shabbes (Yiddish), **Shabbat** (Hebrew): Sabbath.

Shekels: Money. Currently used in Israel.

Shema: The most important Jewish prayer which begins: "Hear, O Israel, the Lord our God, the Lord is One."

Shmattes: Rags. Shabby clothes.

Shmooz: To chat.

Shtetl: The small villages where Jews in Eastern Europe resided for centuries, like those in "Fiddler on the Roof."

Shul: Synagogue, Jewish school, meeting place.

Simchas Torah: Literally the festival of Torah when the final passage of Deuteronomy is chanted and immediately the reading cycle is begun again with the chanting of the first words in Genesis.

Sukkah: A temporary outdoor booth made up of twigs and leaves where meals are eaten during the Feast of Booths (Sukkot). The booths represent the shelters set up by the Jews during the forty years of wandering from Egypt to the Promised Land.

Talmud: A sixty-three book collection of commentaries on the Bible, compiled by Jewish sages. Contains law and lore.

Torah: The Divine Teaching. First five books of the Bible (Genesis, Exodus, Leviticus, Numbers, Deuteronomy).

Yarmulkah: See kipah.

Yeshiva: A school for advanced Jewish studies.

Yiddishkeit: Jewishness. Jewish beliefs and practices.

Yom Kippur: Considered the holiest day of the year for Jews (next to Shabbat). The Day of Atonement.

Appendix B

Worker's Covenant

This was the employee contract between Ellen Kamentsky and Jews for Jesus. It contains statements of theology and employee rules of conduct.

PREAMBLE. Jews for Jesus is an international Jewish evangelistic society and not an organization in the ordinary sense of the word. As a covenant worker I view my role not only as an employee, but also as a fellow minister. The following is a covenant or agreement of principles between co-ministers, based upon the understanding that we are banded together by God for the purpose of serving Y'shua. The purpose of this covenant is to define our mutual commitments in this service. By signing this covenant, I freely agree to abide by its terms.

TITLE I. OUR COMMITMENTS

I set my relationship with God above all other relationships (Romans 12:1-2). Therefore, I promise to conduct myself in all things as befits a child of God (Titus 2:12). I feel the liberty of the Holy Spirit to enter into this colaboring [sic] relationship with Jews for Jesus, understanding that our purpose is to serve God through the preaching of the gospel. I do so in obedience to the Lord, recognizing that part of my responsibility to God is to do the work of Jews for Jesus. I will perform my duties as one entrusted with the things of God. I will guide my behavior, mindful that it reflects my bond with fellow covenant workers.

TITLE II. OUR DUTIES

SECTION A. Attitude.

Our ministry is necessarily difficult and demanding. Occasional hardship is inherent in the lifestyle, and adversity is to be expected in being a witness for Y'shua. I will strive to cultivate an attitude whereby I can accept this as a normal part of my duties. (II Timothy 2:3; Matthew 10:24-25).

SECTION B. Term of Service.

. Jews for Jesus operates on a "term" basis. My term of service is renewable by mutual consent according to the following schedule:

1. First three years--annual renewal
2. Fourth year--triannual renewal
3. After six years--permanent career status, triannual renewal
4. Term of service for a mobile evangelistic team--18 months
5. Covenant renewal is assumed unless notification is given at least 90 days prior to renewal date. Exceptions may be considered on an individual basis.

SECTION C. Work Assignments.

1) AUTHORITY. Authority resides primarily in the executive director of Jews for Jesus who is accountable to the board of directors. Secondarily, authority resides in those whom he appoints to positions of responsibility.

2) ATTITUDE. I agree to accept, in humility, those duties that are assigned by the duly appointed leaders of Jews for Jesus (I Peter 5:5-6). I will try to regard all positions and work assignments with equanimity. I will be required to do work that is both humble and routine. At times I may be required to lead. Insofar as is possible, I will avoid coveting positions of leadership and will fulfill all tasks with diligence, realizing that my enthusiasm is important to the ongoing work of the ministry. If I am given a role whereby I am asked to

lead others, I will always strive to be mindful of their welfare and seek to foster a climate which encourages spiritual growth (Hebrews 13:17; I Timothy 5:17). I will pursue duties diligently and criticize only for the purpose of improving myself and others in their service to God (Hebrews 6:11; II Peter 1:5; Romans 12:10, 16; Thessalonians 5:11, 13). I will neither decline to work nor refuse to interact with any other fellow minister. I will wholeheartedly seek to be forgiven when I've done wrong. When I have been wronged by another, I will wholeheartedly seek to forgive (Ephesians 4:32; I Peter 3:8-9). I agree to accept whatever assignment is made for each term of service with the understanding that reassignments and adjustments in assignment may be made at the discretion of the executive director of Jews for Jesus (Luke 14:11; James 4:10; I Peter 5:6).

3) NOTIFICATION OF INCAPACITY. In the event that there is any change in my ability to perform duties because of emotional, spiritual or physical incapacity, I will notify my immediate supervisor at once. Thereupon, my fitness for service with the ministry may be reviewed by the executive director of Jews for Jesus.

TITLE III. OUR STANDARDS

SECTION A. Doctrinal Statement

1) We believe that the 66 books of the Old and New Testaments are divinely inspired, verbally and completely inerrant in the original writings and of supreme and final authority in all matters of faith and life.

2) We believe in one sovereign God, existing in three persons: Father, Son and Holy Spirit, perfect in holiness, infinite in wisdom, unbounded in power and measureless in love; and that God is the source of all creation and that, through the immediate exercise of His power, all things came into being.

3) We believe that God the Father is the author of eternal salvation, having loved the world and given His Son for its redemption.

4) We believe that Y'shua the Messiah was eternally pre-existent and is co-equal with God the Father; that He took on Himself the nature of mankind through the virgin birth so that He posses both divine and human natures. We believe in His sinless life and perfect obedience to the Law; in His atoning death, burial, bodily resurrection, ascension into heaven, high-priestly intercession and personal return in power and glory.

5) We believe that the Holy Spirit is co-equal and co-eternal with the Father and the Son; that He was active in the creation of all things and continues to be so in providence; that He convicts the world of sin, righteousness and judgement; and that He regenerates, sanctifies, baptizes, indwells, seals, illumines, guides and bestows His gifts upon all believers.

6) We believe that God created man in His image; but that because of the disobedience of our first parents in the Garden of Eden, their innocence was impaired and both they and their descendants, separated from God, suffer physical and spiritual death; and that all human beings, with the exception of Y'shua the Messiah, are sinners by nature and practice.

7) We believe that Y'shua the Messiah died for our sins, according to the Scriptures, as a representative and substitutionary sacrifice; that all who believe in Him are justified, not by any works of righteousness, but by His perfect righteousness and atoning blood; and that there is no other name under heaven by which we must be saved.

8) We believe that Israel exists as a covenant people through whom God continues to accomplish His purposes; and that the Body of the Messiah (the Church) is an elect people in accordance with the New Covenant, compromising both Jews and Gentiles who acknowledge Y'shua as Messiah and Redeemer.

9) We believe that it is permissible for Jewish Christians to observe Jewish cultural traditions, as long as these are not inconsistent with the Word of God or regarded as binding upon the conscience of any person.

10) We believe that Y'shua the Messiah will return personally and bodily in order to consummate the prophesied

purposes concerning His Kingdom.

11) We believe in the bodily resurrection of the just and of the unjust, the everlasting blessedness of the redeemed and the everlasting conscious punishment of the lost. Therefore, we believe in the necessity of preaching the Gospel to Jews and Gentiles.

SECTION B. Doctrinal Questions.
Since people of different doctrinal distinctions are accepted on staff, I will not attempt to persuade any co-workers that their congregational distinctions or doctrinal beliefs are wrong. Honest discussion is encouraged, but I will emphasize only those things that encourage unity and will not claim superiority in those areas which lead to division (II Timothy 2:14; Titus 3:8-9).

SECTION C. Relating to Others.

1) THE LOCAL CONGREGATION. As a group, Jews for Jesus is committed to the biblical position that the local congregation is a representation of the universal body of Messiah (I Corinthians 1:2). It is my personal and spiritual duty to be a part of a local congregation for worship, teaching and fellowship (Hebrews 10:25; Acts 2:41-47). I will affiliate with a congregation that does not conflict with the commitments and doctrinal statement of Jews for Jesus and that upholds me in my ministry. I will be faithful to my congregation, involved in its ministry as much as is practical and generous in my giving (Ephesians 4:11-14; I Corinthians 16:1-2; II Corinthians 9:7, 13-14).

2) THE JEWISH COMMUNITY. I will seek to preserve and maintain my cultural and ethnic heritage in accordance with biblical principles, my conscience and the encouragement of the Jews for Jesus staff. Furthermore, I will participate in Jewish community life as much as is practical and will affirm common values which are compatible with the Scriptures.

3) REPUTATION. The good name and reputation of Jews for Jesus is part of our ability to minister to others. I

agree to conduct myself honorably so that my personal conduct will not detract from that reputation. I will also seek to uphold and protect that reputation. I will avoid entangling Jews for Jesus with my own social and political views. I will not represent myself as a spokesman concerning those issues outside the scope of our doctrinal statement. Since our reputation is reflected in the media, I will consult my supervisor before conducting any interviews. I will not publicly speak against anyone conducting a similar ministry. Those things learned in confidence will remain in confidence, and if I should leave this ministry, I will continue to uphold its reputation and maintain in confidence those things with which I was entrusted.

SECTION D. Appearance.

I will dress and conduct myself in a demeanor that is honoring to the Lord and in modest good taste (I Corinthians 10:31-33; Colossians 3:17, 23; I Timothy 3:12-13, 4:16, 6:11-12, 14). I will avoid questionable forms of amusement (Romans 12:1-2, 13:14, 14:21; Galatians 5:16-25; Ephesians 4:22-24; Colossians 3:1-10; I Peter 1:14-16; I John 2:15-17). If I have any doubt as to the propriety of a given activity, I will consult my supervisor.

SECTION E. Finances.

I will be accorded a lifestyle as supplied by the Lord through my working with Jews for Jesus (I Corinthians 9:13-14; I Timothy 5:8-18). I will not accept any other income for services rendered nor ask for gifts because I am in the ministry (I Thessalonians 5:22; Titus 1:11).

1) GIFTS. I will not encourage personal gifts or gifts which would benefit my ministry (II Corinthians 8:20-21; I Thessalonians 5:22). All gifts given to members of my household resulting from relationships established in the course of my ministry will also be turned over to Jews for Jesus. Any exceptions must be in writing by the executive director. Records of any individual gift must be kept for a

period of three years due to government regulations. This requirement does not pertain to ordinary gifts from family and friends where some reciprocity exists or to modest occasional gifts totalling less than $500 in value per event (e.g. marriage, birth, graduation or new assignment). I may also receive gifts from supporting churches at Christmastime [sic] which are designated "Personal." These gifts should total no more than one half of one month's salary. It is inappropriate to solicit such gifts. I must notify my supervisor if I receive any "personal" gift from a supporter.

2) SUPPLEMENTAL EARNINGS. No staff member may work on any creative project for publication or sale without prior approval. I will turn over to the ministry all royalties, honoraria, talent fees and earnings received from work done during my involvement with Jews for Jesus. These amounts will then go into my account. Royalties and residuals for employment undertaken before I joined the ministry and earnings made from investments do not need to be turned over. In order for the ministry to build the best total benefit package for me, it is suggested that family supplemental earnings be reported.

3) DONOR RELATIONSHIPS. It is my responsibility to build and maintain donor relationships. This provides a base of support for my ministry with Jews for Jesus. I am obligated to build donor relationships for Jews for Jesus rather than for myself. I will encourage donors to give to approved projects and persons. A designated gift for some project which has not been approved cannot be honored and will be returned to the donor. It would be unethical for me, if I were to leave Jews for Jesus and join or form another ministry, to proceed to win donor or church income away from Jews for Jesus. Therefore, if I do leave this ministry, I will not initiate contact with those individuals, pastors or churches from whom I gained support while with Jews for Jesus. Jews for Jesus will supply my name and address to any donor who desires to contact me.

4) STANDARD OF LIVING. While it is the intention

and desire of Jews for Jesus to provide for the needs of the staff, the beginning level of support presumes modest financial obligations on the part of the staff worker. Therefore, those having substantial financial obligations (i.e. extensive family obligations, loans, etc.) will have to do with less and, in some instances, may have to use supplemental sources (e.g. savings) to augment initial living allowances (Timothy 2:3). I will conduct myself in the spirit of Christian sharing, and I can expect my brothers and sisters to share with me (II Corinthians 9:10-11; I Peter 4:9). I will be careful to consider the utilizing of outside resources so as not to elevate my lifestyle too far above that of my co-workers.

5) DEBTS. I should not incur debt in excess of what I can reasonably pay out of current income. I am required to notify my supervisor, in writing, of debts incurred in amounts greater than two months' living allowance, including montages. I am encouraged to discuss finances before incurring such debts. I am not allowed to borrow money from, or loan money to, another co-worker in excess of two days' salary.

SECTION F. Courtship, Marriage and Family Life

1) SELECTION OF MATE. Since it is the nature of the ministry to pervade one's whole life, the wise worker will seek a mate who, by temperament and spirituality, is suited to a ministry commitment. Unmarried staff members and approved students are permitted to contemplate marriage only with believers. Any dating or relationships which might lead to courtship or marriage with nonbelievers will not be tolerated (II Corinthians 6:14-16). It should not be presumed that courtship and marriage are only personal affairs, inasmuch as they greatly affect the course and the conduct of the ministry. Courtship commences when two people choose to explore the possibility of marriage with one another. Therefore, those planning to stay with the ministry must seek counsel and secure consent of their courtship from those in authority

(Hebrews 13:17; I Peter 5:5). The timing of the marriage should be coordinated with the immediate supervisor so that such staff as are needed will be available to be involved in the wedding.

2) DEFINITION OF COURTSHIP. Courtship is a mutual agreement wherein a man and woman relate to one another with a view toward marriage.

3) THE NATURE OF COURTSHIP. Jews for Jesus requires a period of courtship for those contemplating marriage. The courtship may be ended by either party without reason at any time. The staff member(s) involved must notify the ministry of the dissolution of the courtship immediately. Courting couples are special to one another. Therefore, when courting, it is improper to enter into other dating relationships or to allow oneself to contemplate courting another.

4) ASSIGNMENT OF MARRIED PERSONNEL. Assignments will be made on the basis of the skills and qualifications of each individual in a marriage when both persons are involved in the ministry and subject to the Worker's Covenant. However, the talents, abilities and calling of the husband will be given priority consideration when both husband and wife are under the covenant.

5) PREGNANCY. In the event that a married woman in the ministry becomes pregnant, she will offer her resignation as soon as she finds out. Her children are to be considered her first and foremost ministry (Titus 2:4-5). Her status during her pregnancy will be reviewed on a month-to-month basis. Further opportunities for service may be made available at a later date.

6) SINGLES. Jews for Jesus recognizes the validity of a choice to remain single and serve God. We affirm those who choose to remain single in service to Y'shua. The single person who chooses to be single should be shielded from undue pressure to marry (I Corinthians 7:26-7). Those singles who do pursue dating relationships will do so in a responsible manner and in accordance with appropriate dating guidelines. (See Appendix I.)

7) NONEMPLOYED SPOUSES. The nonemployed spouses of Jews for Jesus staff workers are expected to uphold their mates in an unconventional life-style. The ministry will seek to uphold the nonemployed spouses and look for opportunities to involve them in ministry.

8) MARITAL DIFFICULTIES AND DIVORCE. In the event that a married couple should encounter extended marriage difficulties of such a nature that the proper performance of the ministry might possibly be affected, it is the obligation of the head of the family to notify the immediate supervisor at once (I Timothy 3:4-5, 11; I Peter 3:7). In the event that either marriage partner should seek dissolution through unscriptural divorce, the covenant worker must offer his resignation.

9) FAMILY RESPONSIBILITIES. Those members of Jews for Jesus who are single and desire marriage should be given consideration on appointments to place them in positions where they can meet appropriate mates and enter into courtship (Genesis 2:18). Those in a courtship are recognized as requiring consideration in the cultivation of their relationship. Those who are married are entitled to be given assignments which provide for the growth and development of family life (I Corinthians 7:5; Ephesians 5:33). Appointments should be made on the basis of individual merit according to Scripture without respect to gender or marital status (Romans 2:11). It is the duty of the supervisor to encourage good home life. However, there will be times when, for the sake of the ministry, husbands and wives will have to be away from each other. Hopefully, we will not call for extended separation of more than a month at a time unless absolutely necessary for the ongoing work of the ministry (I Corinthians 7:3-5).

SECTION G. Educational Requirements.

I have read the requirements and have met (or will meet) those requirements.

SECTION H. Discipline.

When discipline is required, it is for the furtherance of my ministry (Hebrews 5:8). I will receive it humbly as it is administered through the duly appointed leadership of Jews for Jesus.

SECTION I. Stewardship.

When entrusted with equipment or vehicles owned by Jews for Jesus, I will keep them in good condition. Negligence on my part may incur liability. If negligence reflected in my driving record increases the insurance premiums, I may be asked to pay the difference.

TITLE IV. OUR RIGHTS

SECTION A. The Dignity of the Individual.

1) I bear the image of God and as such deserve to be recognized and treated with respect (Galatians 3:26-28). Accordingly, I have the responsibility to treat others with the same dignity I expect to receive as an equal in Messiah (Matthew 7:12). Every co-minister deserves my full support.

2) I have the right to be given meaningful assignments which are challenging and which utilize my talents and abilities, as well as enable me to develop into a stronger minister. (Ephesians 4:12-13) I also have the right to be consulted with regard to proposed deployment.

SECTION B. Worker's Benefits.

1) GENERAL BENEFITS. I am entitled to certain employee benefits which will be determined by the board of directors. These include life insurance, dental and hospital insurance, provision for retirement, stated vacation time, sick leave, education and travel benefits, and others as may be appointed. Concerning retirement, benefit packages may differ with terms of service.

2) TRANSFER. In the case of required transfer, the least amount of family and financial disruption will be sought. If

the ministry has approved the purchase of a home, then requires a transfer within two years of that purchase and if after reasonable attempt to sell the property, a loss is incurred, Jews for Jesus will endeavor to make up that loss less reasonable rental rate.

3) EDUCATION. I am entitled as part of my service to gain additional education in an approved course of study to better myself for service. However, such education must not interfere with the ability to do routine duties (II Peter 1:2, 3:18).

4) CHILDREN. The ministry, in partnership with me, will take an interest in providing a proper spiritual education for my children.

a) In certain instances, my children may receive scholarships to aid and encourage that education provided the school does meet ministry standards. (See Appendix II.)

b) Staff workers' children who are attending Christian college or seminary for the purpose of preparing for Christian service may be granted a scholarship whether or not they plan to work with Jews for Jesus.

5) SENIORITY & MERITORIOUS SERVICE. I am entitled to seniority considerations and meritorious service commendation review in the making of future deployments. If I am one who has given much to the Jews for Jesus organization, I should be entitled to more consideration, benefits and deployments than newcomers (Hebrews 6:10). Since benefits are commensurate with responsibility borne, benefits may change with changes in responsibility.

SECTION C. Conflict Arbitration

1) ACCESS TO PERSONAL FILES. While in service with Jews for Jesus, I am entitled to know all matters held in my file which might affect my career or service with the ministry, whether they be reports of merit or complaint. If an accusation is brought against me, I am entitled to face my accuser. Anonymous accusations will not be received (Luke 3:14; I Timothy 5:19; I Peter 3:16).

2) RIGHTS OF REDRESS.

a) I have the right to receive clear communication of what is expected of me. Every relationship or assignment can proceed smoothly only on the basis of clearly stated directives, goals and information. If I am confused about my relationship or assignment, or discover that misunderstanding exists, I am responsible to ask for clarification. Written communication of assignments is encouraged so as to reduce misunderstanding and to aid in the process of reconciliation or adjudication.

b) In the event that I feel that I have been dealt with unjustly, I have the right to seek redress. First, I must have exhausted every possible means of redemptively dealing with my supervisor with whom I have the grievance. I will not make common cause of my problem among fellow workers. If I have a grievance with a co-worker or my supervisor, I will not discuss that grievance with anyone outside the ministry except my family, pastor or professional counselor (Ephesians 4:29-32; Colossians 3:9-10, 13-14). Any action of mine which spreads a spirit of dissension or which seeks to align sympathy for me against another person will have the affect of weakening my case when it is reviewed. Further, my case should not be taken above my supervisor without his or her knowledge except in the case of moral turpitude.

c) My appeal for redress must be made after giving notice of intent with a bill of particulars to my supervisor. If I have exhausted every possible means of dealing redemptively with my supervisor my appeal is then to the next step up on the chain of authority (Matthew 18:15-16). The next step would be either a branch leader or the executive director, depending on who supervises my leader. If my appeal goes beyond the mediation of the executive director it will then be presented to the Jews for Jesus Council for arbitration. The final step in the chain of command is the president of the board of directors who may then appoint two board members who are not employees of Jews for Jesus. One shall be designated chairman and shall be responsible to arrange a meeting between the two board members and all parties involved in the complaint as soon as possible. The board representatives shall be responsible to ascertain the full nature of the problem to the best of their ability, to make recommendations for the resolution of the problem directly to the parties involved, to report proceedings in full to the board, and to make any recommendations to the board which they consider necessary (Galatians 6:1-2). In that the board of directors is the highest level of appeal, I agree to accept the decision of the board as final.

d) I understand that in the event of an accident or a grievance I will not institute a lawsuit against any staff worker or the ministry, but will seek Christian arbitration through a mutually agreeable third party (I Corinthians 6:1-8).

SECTION D. Leaving the Ministry

1) RESIGNATION. Since I am not an employee in the ordinary sense of the word, it is inherent in the covenant to facilitate leaving the ministry of Jews for Jesus should I no longer feel the liberty of the Holy Spirit to renew my covenant relationship. To make this transition as orderly as possible I will give at least 90 days notice of my intent not to renew my covenant prior to any renewal date. Should I reapply in the future, my abilities, capabilities and longevity will be considered in the re-establishment of my benefits package. I might not return to the same position I held when I left. If I leave before my term is finished without the expressed prior consent of the Jews for Jesus Council, I cannot expect to receive a positive reference or letter of recommendation from Jews for Jesus. Any reference given on my behalf will always include the phrase that I did not fulfill the terms of my agreement.

2) LEAVE OF ABSENCE. Should a leave of absence be necessary, it will be reviewed in quarterly segments up to one full year. If I do not return to Jews for Jesus after one year I will be considered as having resigned. Certain benefits may be extended to me during my leave of absence as reviewed by the executive director of Jews for Jesus.

3) SUSPENSION. If it is determined that I am not fulfilling my duty, I may be suspended from those duties. This will be reviewed by the executive director of Jews for Jesus, and should I not find other employment during my suspension, certain benefits may be extended to me including salary or health benefits from the funds which I have raised.

4) DISMISSAL. In the event that I am dismissed from my post of service for any reason except dishonesty or moral turpitude, I may have the equivalent of living allowance through the end of my term. This allowance will be received provided there are sufficient funds in my account and there is no other employment or occupation.

TITLE V. AMENDING THIS COVENANT

No change can be made to this covenant without a three-fourths majority vote of the board of directors of Jews for Jesus.

____________________	____________________
Executive Director	Covenant Worker
____________________	____________________
Date	Date

APPENDIX I

Dating Guidelines

The following is a list of guidelines for single staff workers who choose to enter into a dating relationship.

1. Staff workers do not need permission to date.

2. Staff workers should not date people who are a part of their "caseload."

3. Dating or courting couples should not entertain one another alone in their respective places of residence.

4. A dating couple should not go on vacation together or take weekends away together unless the event is structured and chaperoned (e.g. a singles weekend). Thus, traveling together unaccompanied is not acceptable. Going to motels together, even if you are staying in separate rooms, should not occur.

5. No staff worker should pursue an extended relationship or courtship with more than one person at a time.

6. No staff worker should date a nonbeliever.

7. Staff workers should not date someone who is separated or in the process of divorce.

8. Staff workers who have a ministry career mind-set should try to seek a mate who is like-minded.

9. Before dating a nonstaff person, a vocational worker should seriously consider the possible consequences of that relationship:

   a. It is possible that the nonstaff person will not understand the lifestyle inherent with a ministry commitment and thus make unreasonable demands of the worker's time and energy.

b. The staff worker might become distracted from his ministry duties and readjust his priorities inappropriately.

c. If the dating relationship were to end in an unfriendly way, the nonstaff person might cease attending ministry functions.

10. In courtship one must remember that families are involved. Couples seeking engagement should plan to meet and spend time with each other's respective parents while the other person is not present. This will enable the individual to get to know the parents in a way that would not be possible if the couple were together.

APPENDIX II

School Standards

1. Orthodoxy: The school should have a doctrinal statement available which agrees in principle with that of the Jews for Jesus ministry. Where none is offered, the headmaster and the main teacher must state their written agreement with the doctrinal statement of Jews for Jesus.

In general, the school must be recognized in the local Christian community as upholding the evangelical position.

2. Tuition Benefit: The actual amount of the benefit is to be determined by the executive director of Jews for Jesus. It will be a significant portion of the tuition and registration fees (where applied).

3. Quality: The school must be accredited by the state in which it is located or by recognized, standard accrediting agencies.

The school may not practice racial segregation and should represent various socio-economic classes. It should be operated as a non-profit organization and must show intent to teach the Christian faith to all children enrolled.

Appendix C

Resource Organizations

American Family Foundation
P.O. Box 2265
Bonita Springs, FL 33959
(212) 249-7693

Cult Awareness Network
National Office
2421 West Pratt Blvd., Suite 1173
Chicago, IL 60645
(312) 267-7777

International Cult Education Program
P.O. Box 1232, Gracie Station
New York, NY 10028
(212) 439-1550

Jewish Board of Family and Children's Services
Cult Hotline and Clinic
120 West 57th St.
New York, NY 10019
(212) 632-4640

Jewish Community Relations Council of New York
Task Force on Missionaries and Cults
711 Third Ave., 12th floor
New York, NY 10017
(212) 983-4800